The Little Bubishi

A History of Karate for Children

By Andrew O'Brien
Illustrations by Emma O'Brien

Eloquent Books

Copyright 2010
All rights reserved — Andrew O'Brien

No part of this book may be reproduced or transmitted in any form or by any means, graphic, electronic, or mechanical, including photocopying, recording, taping, or by any information storage retrieval system, without the permission, in writing, from the publisher.

Eloquent Books
An imprint of Strategic Book Group
P.O. Box 333
Durham CT 06422
www.StrategicBookGroup.com

ISBN: 978-1-60911-717-7

Printed in the United States of America

For my big sister Lee, the most courageous person I've ever known

How we miss you

Contents

Acknowledgments vii
Introduction ix
Chapter 1—Okinawa and the Birth of Karate-Do 2
Chapter 2—What Does 'Bubishi' Mean? 4
Chapter 3—A Definition of 'Karate-Do' 5
Chapter 4—Kata. 7
Chapter 5—Fact or Fantasy? 9
Chapter 6—Bodhidharma—The Young Prince 12
Chapter 7—The Monk Prince 14
Chapter 8—Meeting the Emperor 16
Chapter 9—The Shaolin Monastery. 18
Chapter 10—The Ghost of Bodhidharma 20
Chapter 11—Qiniang Fang—Zhonghong Fang's Escape 22
Chapter 12—A Man's Responsibility 24
Chapter 13—Zhonghong's Vow 28
Chapter 14—Qiniang's World Is Shattered 30
Chapter 15—Qiniang and the White Cranes 32
Chapter 16—The Importance of Qiniang Fang 36
Chapter 17—Satunushi 'Tode' Sakugawa—The Petulant Youth 37
Chapter 18—'Tode' 40
Chapter 19—A New Teacher 41
Chapter 20—A Lesson in Night Fighting 43
Chapter 21—What a Relief 45
Chapter 22—Todes's Pirate Adventure 47
Chapter 23—The Importance of Tode Sakugawa 51
Chapter 24—Sokon 'Bushi' Matsumura—Matsumura and Tode 52

Chapter 25—Sokon 'Bushi' Matsumura—Royal Protector. 54
Chapter 26—If Looks Could Kill. 56
Chapter 27—Bushi the Bullfighter 62
Chapter 28—Matsumura and Chinto. 68
Chapter 29—The Importance of Matsumura. 73
Chapter 30—Yasutsune 'Anko' Itosu the Powerhouse 74
Chapter 31—Itosu Takes the Bull by the Horns 76
Chapter 32—Pick on Someone Your Own Age. 81
Chapter 33—Old Itosu and the Judo Master 85
Chapter 34—The Importance of Itosu 88
Chapter 35—Itosu's Ten Precepts of China Hand. 90
Chapter 36—Yasutsune Azato—the Mysterious Master. 93
Chapter 37—With Hands Mightier Than a Sword. 95
Chapter 38—The Importance of Azato 100
Chapter 39—Gichin Funakoshi—An Eventful Year. 101
Chapter 40—Azato's Amazing Offer 103
Chapter 41—Nosey Neighbours 105
Chapter 42—Do It Again, Funakoshi! 107
Chapter 43—Fighting a Typhoon 109
Chapter 44—Time for Change. 117
Chapter 45—No Need for Violence. 119
Chapter 46—Gichin Funakoshi's Twenty Precepts of Karate-Do. 126
Chapter 47—Gichin Funakoshi—The Father of Modern Karate-Do . . . 139
Chapter 48—Modern Masters—You Could Be One! 143
Chapter 49—Practical Self-Protection for the Whole Family 146
Chapter 50—Karate Terminology 149
Chapter 51—Dojo Etiquette/Rules. 156
Bibliography & Further Reading 159

Acknowledgments

To my mum and dad for creating me – you did well, although I might be biased; my little sister, Samantha and her partner Sir John! To my beautiful and talented daughters Emma and Abbie, I love you both. To any man lucky enough to have a relationship with either of them – I'm watching you! Thanks to Robert, my stepdad, for the innumerable ways he has helped our family, and to Rachel for keeping Dad young.

Now to my great Karate influences and heroes: firstly, and definitely most importantly, my dad Mike O'Brien, 8th Dan, 'The Father of Welsh Karate'; Sensei Andy Sherry; 'The Tiger of Shotokan Karate', Sensei Keinosuke Enoeda; Bruce Lee, the man who has probably influenced practically every martial artist since the 1970s; Sensei Dave Hazard, as far as I and many others are concerned, the finest exponent of Shotokan Karate in the world today bar none; my good friend and fellow KUW instructor Stuart Jenkins, who has encouraged and influenced my Karate more than he realizes; Iain Abernethy, the best bunkai man in the business and a gentleman to boot; Geoff Thompson, whose life story encouraged me to put pen to paper; Shaun and Emma of The Shotokan Way for all their support over the past few years. For all of my students past and present, a huge thanks to you too.

Paul, Scott, Martyn and everyone at Regional Mortgage Services Ltd, I'd like to thank you for nine years of enjoyable and memorable employment but, quite perversely, I'd like to extend even more thanks for making me redundant in 2008. Redundancy brought with it the time and opportunity to write this book. To my life-long friend Richard Hughes, who has propped me up through many difficult times and without whose advice and support this book would not have been published. A big thank you also to Amanda Burfoot, my first ever editor, for her expertise and patience.

Finally, Eleri, my best friend, soulmate and love of my life. Without her endless encouragement and unwavering belief in me, I would never have written down one word. I intend to spend the rest of my life thanking you.

Introduction

I consider myself to be a very lucky man. Born in Cardiff, the capital city of Wales, on 14th January 1967, I was the second of three children and only son to Michael and Doreen O'Brien. As fate would have it, my father just happened to be the first ever Welshman to attain the coveted black belt in a new sporting phenomenon that was sweeping across the world at that time. That phenomenon was Karate-Do or, more specifically for me, Shotokan Karate-Do.

I have vivid memories from my early childhood of eagerly watching Dad practising his Karate in the garden or the living room (much to my mother's annoyance!) and even more vivid memories of walking into one of his reverse kicks when he wasn't aware of my presence. It sent me flying into the kitchen, where I landed in a tearful heap, which didn't do much to endear my mother to Dad training in the house!

On special occasions, if I had been well behaved (or if Dad wanted to stay in Mam's good books), Dad would take me along to his dojo to watch one of his classes, where I was tolerated by his very patient students. After all, it is very difficult for a two-year-old toddler to sit still and be silent for up to three hours. The dojo was located above my uncle's print shop in the heart of Cardiff's dockland, which had the reputation of being quite a rough area at that time. The dojo lived up to that reputation both in appearance and in the context of the training.

I can clearly remember the Japanese 'Rising Sun' flag hanging on the wall next to a large portrait of Gichin Funakoshi, The Father of Modern Karate-Do, before which everyone knelt and bowed before and after training. The dilapidated dojo had holes in the ceiling, which allowed water to pour in when it rained. This would then be caught in buckets and bowls that were dotted around the rough floorboards. That fantastic room where the spirit of Karate first touched and took hold of me was freezing in the winter, stiflingly hot in the summer, wet when it rained, and dusty and dirty when it was dry. I absolutely loved it!

Then, one evening, I was sitting with my mother waiting for Dad to leave for his class when he came into the living room with his hands hidden behind his back.

"Andy, come here, son. I've got something for you," he said.

As I approached him, he revealed what he was hiding, and a huge rush of excitement shuddered through my entire body. In his hands he held my first brand new, dazzling white Karate uniform (gi). That was thirty-eight years ago; I was four years old and I've never looked back.

In 1978, at the age of eleven, I received my 1st Dan black belt from the legendary Japanese karateka Sensei Keinosuke Enoeda, becoming at that time one of the youngest karateka in Great Britain to receive that honour. It was around then that I started to browse through the substantial library of martial arts books that my father had by now amassed.

They contained fantastic pictures of amazing karateka performing incredible techniques, which I loved to study and try to emulate. Most of them had originally been written in Japanese and then translated into English, but unfortunately, for an eleven-year-old, the language used in the translation was often confusing and, if I'm totally honest, pretty boring too. As I've grown older I've inherited, bought, and come to love and cherish those very same books that I found so difficult to read as a child.

What about you, though, the children and young adults of today who are the future of Karate-Do and indeed the world? Many books have been written on the subject of Karate, but the vast majority of them are still directed at adults and old fogies like me.

As an instructor to hundreds of children and teenagers over the past twenty-five years or more, I have had to devise many methods to maintain the attention and interest of my younger members, with storytelling being a huge favourite with them all. The amazing tales of the great Karate Masters enthused and encouraged many of them to train harder and some of them to stay in the art for life.

For many people, Karate is simply what they see in tournaments or on the big screen, but it is so much more. Yes, it is a fighting art, but studied in its entirety it promotes a better way of life, and taught properly it moulds and nurtures good, honest, and decent human beings.

The Little Bubishi tells some of the fantastic tales and legends of just a few of my favourite martial artists and karateka from history. It explains the part they played in bringing Karate out of a veil of secrecy and illegality, eventually making it one of the biggest participant sports the world has ever seen. It also deals with the philosophies of Karate in a way that children can understand and relate to.

Although this book is aimed at children and teenagers, the stories are ideal for adults to both read to younger children and enjoy themselves. Whether you are a student of Karate or not, my hope is that this book will encourage those that are to stay in their chosen art for life, and for those who are not, children and adults alike, to be motivated to at least try this life-enhancing pastime.

I sincerely hope that you enjoy reading *The Little Bubishi* as much as I have enjoyed writing it.

Part I

The Origins of Karate-Do

1
Okinawa and the Birth of Karate-Do

Without delving too deeply into the complicated history of Karate-Do, I think that it's important that you get just a little background into the events that brought the martial arts and, in particular, Karate-Do into being. As your interest develops for this fascinating subject, you may want to investigate it further. Some of my favourite books on the subject are listed in the Bibliography at the end of the book.

In around the year 1500, the King of Okinawa, Sho Shin, declared the carrying of all weapons illegal to stop feuding warlords from fighting each other. All weapons were confiscated and stored in a large warehouse. A long period of peace and prosperity began for the people of Okinawa.

Then, in 1609, the Satsuma samurai clan, armed with swords and firearms, invaded Okinawa from Kyushu in Southern Japan. For the first time in over a century, the people of Okinawa took up arms to protect their homes. Despite their brave efforts, the highly trained samurai swiftly defeated them. The new rulers of Okinawa once again outlawed the carrying of weapons, a law that remained in force for another two hundred and fifty years.

Without weapons, the Uchinanchu (Okinawan people) had to develop a means of defending themselves against thugs and ruffians. By using farm implements, long staffs (bo) and empty-hand techniques combined with the strong influence of the Chinese and Japanese fighting arts, Okinawa became the birthplace of Karate-Do.

2
What Does 'Bubishi' Mean?

The Japanese word 'Bubishi' means 'Book of Military Preparation'. The *Bubishi* is a book thought to have been brought to Okinawa from China and contains diagrams and text showing fighting techniques, special pressure points on the body that can both kill and heal a person, herbal medicines, and historical information.

The contents of The *Bubishi* were kept highly secret for many, many years and only ever passed on to a single student by its keeper. Then, in 1936, Mabuni Kenwa, the founder of a style of Karate called Shito Ryu, made The *Bubishi* of his great Master Yasutsune 'Anko' Itosu public for the very first time.

The *Bubishi* is now widely regarded as the 'Bible of Karate' from which all Karate today is derived.

3
A Definition of 'Karate-Do'

Kara (空) = Empty Te (手) = Hand Do (道) = Way

Karate-Do 空手道 The Way of the Empty Hand

The original Chinese character for 'Kara'— 唐 —means 'Chinese', and the character 'te'— 手 —means 'hand'. The Chinese character was used due to the strong cultural influence China had on Okinawa for many centuries. So at the time, Karate meant 'Chinese Hand', also known on Okinawa as 'To-de' or 'Toudi'.

By the early 20th century, Okinawa had been part of Japan for some time and Karate-Do was being openly taught on the Japanese mainland. For these reasons, the Japanese character for 'Kara' 空, meaning 'empty', replaced the original Chinese version. This was to make it more acceptable, understandable, and respectful to the Japanese. So To-de (Chinese Hand) finally became Karate (Empty Hand).

Many of the Chinese kata names were also given Japanese versions so that they would make sense in Japanese schools and universities, where Karate was now being taught as part of the curriculum. The Japanese government believed that Karate would make their children fit and strong for their armed forces.

4
Kata

Throughout this book you will see the term 'kata' referred to regularly. The word 'kata' means 'form', and in Japan is a very important ideal, as it relates to many areas of Japanese life and not just Karate.

Kata in Japan could be described as traditional rituals or 'shikata' (the correct way of doing things), and can apply to simple everyday matters. For instance, the Japanese have applied kata to reading, writing, eating, dressing, and even making tea.

For many decades, Karate on Okinawa was shrouded in secrecy and even forbidden, so no written or pictorial records were kept. For this reason, the great Masters of Karate had to create Karate kata to enable them to remember and pass on their knowledge to their students.

They arranged the fighting systems into groups of techniques performed in a set pattern that generally begin and end on the same spot. In this respect, kata are very much like dances, but dances with lethal intent! As a matter of fact, fighting techniques were often hidden within the folk dances of Okinawa.

There are about twenty-six Karate kata practised today depending on which school of Karate you belong to. Karate kata progress from quite simple forms for beginners to very complex and difficult forms for the more experienced karateka (a person who practises Karate).

It is essential that once a kata has been learned correctly, the 'bunkai', or true use and analysis of the techniques in real combat, are also understood. As The Father of Modern Karate-Do, Gichin Funakoshi wrote in his book *Karate-Do: My Way of Life*:

> *"You may train for a long, long time, but if you merely move your hands and feet and jump up and down like a puppet, learning Karate is not very different from learning to dance."*

5
Fact or Fantasy?

The incredible stories of Karate-Do and its legendary Masters are steeped in myth, mystery, fable, and fantasy as well as fact. Stories of incredible heroism and amazing superhuman feats are interwoven with the truth of the very real and equally heroic dedication and hard work required to become a true Karate Master.

The stories of the great past Masters of Karate may seem exaggerated and hard to believe. A reason for this may be that back then, as now, students would often stretch the truth of their Master's ability and adventures to make them appear more accomplished and braver than a rival's Master; a case of 'my teacher's better than your teacher'. On the other hand, we weren't there, so for all we know these fantastic tales may well be true. I like to think so.

One thing is absolutely for sure, though: the dedicated, inspirational, and pioneering hard work of the great Masters of the martial arts and Karate-Do has inspired generations of boys and girls to take up a fighting art. Now, Karate, which was once a mysterious fighting system practised in secret on a tiny island in the East China Sea, has millions of participants all over the world.

Their fantastic stories of steely determination, dedication, and bravery have elevated these great men to legendary status.

Part II

The Amazing Adventures of Karate-Do's Legendary Masters

6
Bodhidharma—The Young Prince

A very, very long time ago, in fact over fifteen hundred years ago, a child was born in the mystical country of India. His father, who was king of a huge jungle province, was overjoyed at the birth of his third son, who soon became his favourite and the heir to the throne.

As he grew up, it became clear that the young prince was very different to his brothers. He was not interested in all the wealth and privilege that being part of the royal family brought. He was a very intelligent and extremely inquisitive boy who preferred to spend his time wandering in the jungle observing and studying the incredible wildlife that lived there. Hour upon hour he would spend hidden in trees or behind bushes watching the tigers, monkeys, snakes, birds, and crocodiles, and how they hunted prey, fought off danger, and loved and cared for their young.

When he was alone in the palace, the young prince would mimic his favourite animals. He would copy their sounds, facial expressions and movements; the tiger's stealthy stalking and explosive attacking power, the monkey's hysterical acrobatics and antics, the lightning speed of the snake's venomous strike and the ferocious whipping action of the crocodile's tail.

The young prince did this so often that after several years he became as strong and as agile, as fast and as graceful, as ferocious a fighter and as tender and loving as the animals he so admired. He also had a wild animal-like look about him with his long black hair and extremely wide, staring eyes.

Coupled with these animalistic skills, the young prince had also practised and become a great master of the ancient Indian fighting art of 'Kalaripayattu'. So despite his gentle manner and peaceful ways, the young Indian prince was also a fearsome warrior. Kalaripayattu is thought to be one of the oldest martial arts in the world and uses swords, shields, sticks, and empty-hand techniques.

7
The Monk Prince

By the time he was a young man, the Prince had reached a very important decision about the direction in which he wanted to take his life. He went to his father and told him that he no longer wished to be a prince and that he was giving up all of his royal privileges to become a Buddhist monk. Buddhism reveres and cares for all living things, just as he did, and he wanted to teach others about his beliefs. The King was not at all surprised by his beloved son's decision and gave him his blessing to follow his heart and become a monk.

The Prince became a disciple of Prajnatara, who was a very rare person indeed in that she was a female Buddhist said to have reached enlightenment. Under her guidance, the Prince studiously and conscientiously threw himself into his chosen life. He meditated for hour upon hour, studied and memorized Buddhist scrolls and maintained his physical fitness through his martial arts training.

So great was his devotion to Buddhism that after many years, Prajnatara declared that he was truly enlightened. Prajnatara then gave him the name Bodhidharma and ordered him to travel east to the mysterious land of China. There he was to meet the Emperor and teach the Buddhist monks of China how a state of enlightenment may be achieved through devotion and hard work.

Before I tell you of Bodhidharma's journey and adventures in China, perhaps I should try to explain to you what enlightenment is. Enlightenment is achieved using meditation, concentrating very hard to empty the mind of all thoughts. If you think that sounds easy, try it now.

Close your eyes and try not to think of anything at all. Did you try? Did you manage not to think of anything? I bet something just popped in there, didn't it! Now you can see how difficult it really is. If a Buddhist reaches enlightenment, for most do not, it is said that he or she understands everything about life and death and allows no bad or negative thoughts into his or her mind.

8
Meeting the Emperor

For three long years, wearing nothing but his humble black monk's robes and only sandals on his feet, Bodhidharma trekked across the mighty snow-covered Himalayas and sailed the stormy seas. Through freezing cold winds and blinding blizzards, through squally seas with crashing waves five times taller than his ship, Bodhidharma battled onwards. It is believed that he finally arrived in China in September of the year 527, when his ship sailed into Canton harbour.

His meeting with the Emperor did not go well at all, though. The Emperor was taken aback and intimidated at the travel-beaten appearance of Bodhidharma. His wild wide eyes and tattered robes gave him quite a terrifying appearance, which scared the finely dressed and vainly manicured Emperor and his courtiers.

To make matters worse, the Emperor then asked Bodhidharma what his reward in the afterlife would be for promoting Buddhism throughout China. "After all, I am building monasteries and erecting images of Buddha all over China," the Emperor bragged.

Bodhidharma was furious and curtly replied, "Your reward will be nothing! Spreading the word of Buddha to your fellow man is reward in itself. If you do not understand this you will never become enlightened."

9
The Shaolin Monastery

Disheartened by the Emperor's attitude, Bodhidharma left the palace and continued his journey northwards to the Chinese province of Henan. There he discovered the beautiful Shaolin (Small Forest) Monastery on Mount Shaoshi. Bodhidharma was awed by the beauty of the temple. With its beautiful main gate guarded by stone lions and the awe-inspiring pagoda gardens, he was sure it was the most incredible monastery he had ever seen. Unfortunately, his initial thrill and excitement was to be short-lived.

The Shaolin monks did not have his high standards of discipline and they would often fall asleep during meditation. It was also a monk's duty to go into the community and spread the word of Buddha amongst the people. However, the Shaolin monks were so weak and defenceless that they were afraid to venture outside the monastery walls for fear of being attacked by the ruthless bandits that roamed the countryside.

Bodhidharma immediately set about instructing the Shaolin monks in physical training, fighting skills, ways of discipline, and meditation techniques. He was a strict taskmaster and made the monks train hard from sunrise to sunset. This incredibly tough and gruelling regime was to pave the way for the future of the Chinese fighting arts.

After three years of constant and very demanding training, the monks were so physically fit, strong, and amazingly skilled martial artists that the bandits would not dare try to attack them. The monks could now go into the community with confidence.

His work done, Bodhidharma then retired to a nearby cave, where he sat facing a wall and meditated for nine whole years! During the seventh year, legend tells us that he fell asleep and was so angry with himself that he tore out his eyelashes to teach his eyes a lesson.

The lashes fell to the ground and plants sprouted from where they landed. The Shaolin monks then picked leaves from the plants and made tea from them, which has helped to keep them awake during meditation ever since.

There is another, more gruesome version of this tale. Instead of his eyelashes, Bodhidharma is said to have actually cut his eyelids off so that he could never fall asleep again. The tea plants sprouted from the earth where the severed eyelids landed. I think I prefer the first version!

10
The Ghost of Bodhidharma

Bodhidharma is said to have died at the incredibly old age of one hundred and fifty. Three years after he died, a very curious thing happened indeed. A man who knew Bodhidharma very well claimed to have seen him trekking back over the Himalayan Mountains. The man also claimed that the long-dead Bodhidharma was walking barefoot and carrying one sandal.

Understandably shocked and just a little frightened, the man ran back to the Shaolin Monastery to tell the monks what he had seen. There was only one way to find out for sure if his story was true. They would have to open Bodhidharma's tomb. With bated breath and rapidly beating hearts, they prised open the tomb and sure enough all they found was a sealed iron chest and a single sandal. There was no trace of Bodhidharma's body!

Curiosity getting the better of them, the monks resealed the tomb but kept the iron chest to find out what was inside. When they opened it, they found two books written by Bodhidharma. One has long been lost and nobody really knows what story it told. The other, called the *Yi Jin Jing* (*Muscle Changing Classic*), contained diagrams of Bodhidharma's physical exercises and fighting techniques. The Shaolin monks kept the *Yi Jin Jing* secret for hundreds of years, and it is believed by some that by studying Bodhidharma's diagrams, they were able to develop their now famous styles of Chuan Fa, better known as Kung Fu.

Although much of Bodhidharma's story is known to be true, the development of the Shaolin monks' styles of Kung Fu as a direct result of Bodhidharma's teachings or the discovery of the *Yi Jin Jing* may or may not have actually happened, and has been the subject of much debate.

Whether the story is true or not, the Indian monk prince, Bodhidharma, will be forever linked to the Shaolin Monastery and the creation of the Chinese martial arts. As you will now discover, the styles of Kung Fu created and developed in the Shaolin Temple were to have a great influence on the creation of Karate-Do.

11
Qiniang Fang–Zhonghong Fang's Escape

After the death of Bodhidharma, the years, decades, and centuries came and went, and the Shaolin monks became famous throughout China for their fighting skills and styles. Then, in the 1600s, during the Qing Dynasty, there was great unrest throughout China and many people were opposed to the Emperor and his laws.

The Shaolin Monastery became a safe haven for rebels fighting against the Emperor's troops. When word of this got to the Emperor, he was furious, and in the year 1674 he ordered his army to attack the monastery and slaughter everyone found within it. During the attack many of the monks were brutally murdered and the beautiful monastery was burned to the ground.

Miraculously, not everyone was killed, and amongst those who were able to escape the slaughter was a great Master of the Shaolin art of Eighteen Monk Fist Boxing, Zhonghong Fang. He made his escape during the attack on the temple and travelled for many weeks in search of sanctuary. Begging for food and shelter, he eventually arrived in the province of Fujian on the coast of the South China Sea and settled in the small village of Yongchun near Fuzhou.

The villagers immediately took a liking to the polite and kindly stranger and made him very welcome. As his reputation for being kind, wise, and a great martial artist spread amongst the villagers, Zhonghong soon became an important figure and leader in his new home. Zhonghong Fang soon met, fell in love with, and married his wife, and before very long she gave birth to a beautiful baby girl, whom they named Qiniang.

12
A Man's Responsibility

Before Zhonghong's arrival, the villagers of Yongchun had been having a lot of trouble with young ruffians from a neighbouring village. Travelling in drunken gangs, they would come to Yongchun at night to bully, intimidate, and steal from the peaceful villagers. Zhonghong, being a great negotiator, was asked to travel to the other village and speak to its elders. He asked them if they would take control of the actions of their young men. He identified the troublemakers, who were then punished and banned from drinking alcohol, and for some time the trouble stopped.

Then, one beautiful, serenely peaceful summer's evening, Qiniang was quietly playing outside her house under the watchful eye of her mother, who was chopping wood for the fire. Qiniang paused for a moment when she heard the distant sound of men talking very loudly. She could hear them swearing and laughing hysterically. Slowly and surely, the voices seemed to be getting closer, and the child's mother could also now hear their unsavoury language above the thud of the falling axe.

Realizing there could be trouble brewing, Qiniang's mother gathered up the firewood and shouted for her daughter to get inside the house as quickly as possible. It was too late; before they could get into the safety of their house, three very drunk and rowdy youths came round a bend in the road and spotted the wife and child of Zhonghong. This was an opportunity too good to miss for the boozy bunch of thugs. They were determined to exact revenge upon the interfering old man that had got them punished, and having some fun with his wife and daughter would be a great start.

One of the thugs grabbed the tiny and terrified Qiniang by her hair and began shaking and dragging her around like a fox would a rabbit. The poor child could do nothing but hold onto her head and cry and plead for the cowardly youth to let her go.

Seeing Qiniang in such distress enraged her mother so much that she fought her way out of the grip of the two brutes tearing at her clothes. She ran and grabbed a large stick from the strewn pile of firewood and she struck Qiniang's attacker across the back of the head, instantly knocking him unconscious.

One of the other men ran and tackled her. Pulling the stick from her grip, he held her arms behind her back with one hand and took hold of her hair with the other. He turned to the third man and sniggered. "She likes a fight, so let's give her a fight," he said.

The other man grinned as he walked up to the woman. He came so close that she could smell his foul, alcohol-reeking breath. "You are going to pay for that," he hissed at her, spraying saliva in her face as he pointed to his unconscious cohort. He raised his right arm across his body in preparation to strike her with the back of his hand.

"Run, Qiniang!" she cried. "Get your father!" But Qiniang was frozen in terror at the dreadful sight before her. "Qiniang, please… RUN!"

CRACK! Qiniang saw the back of the thug's hand viciously swipe across her mother's face and blood begin pouring from her mouth.

The youth turned to Qiniang, gave her an evil grin, and cruelly mimicked the child's mother, saying, "Run, Qiniang, run." Then both men burst into drunken, high-pitched, hyena-like laughter, and returned their attentions to the now semi-conscious woman.

Coming to her senses and realizing what she must do, Qiniang ran screaming at the top of her voice towards the village hall where her father was at a meeting with the other men. She was only half way there when her father and his friends came running towards her. Her cries for help had been so loud that the men had heard her and immediately abandoned the meeting to find out what was going on.

Scooping Qiniang up in his arms and kissing her tiny, tear-soaked face, Zhonghong, along with the other men, sprinted back to his home. His heart was ripped in two at the sight of his wife lying sobbing in the yard, her clothes torn and her face bloody and beaten. The two low-life cowards could be heard ransacking the house.

Several of the men charged towards the door, ready to deliver swift justice for their dear friend and his family.

"No!" Fang exclaimed. Calmly handing his quivering child to a friend, he said, "It's a man's responsibility to protect his family. I'll deal with them." After kneeling to kiss his wife, he calmly and confidently disappeared into his house.

Now, you would expect that a great fight ensued, taking many minutes, with Zhonghong Fang possibly receiving a terrible beating, as he was tackling two much younger men. Do not forget, though, that both the thugs were very much the worse for wear from the alcohol they had consumed and greatly underestimated their older opponent, which is a mistake often made by young men.

Less than thirty seconds later, Zhonghong emerged from the house, dragging both men, who were now unconscious, by their collars, and he laid them neatly face down in the dirt beside the man his wife had knocked out. Qiniang, overjoyed that her father was safe, ran to him, and throwing her arms around his waist, she buried her head in his arms and began to sob uncontrollably.

"There, there, my love. They cannot hurt you now. I will never leave you alone again and from now on I will always be here to protect you both," he gently whispered in her ear as a tear rolled down his cheek into his beloved Qiniang's silky black hair.

13
Zhonghong's Vow

The three thugs were rudely awakened from their enforced slumber by an ice-cold bucket of water thrown over them by Zhonghong. Their heads were thumping painfully, partly due to the severe beating they had taken at the hands of the older man, and partly to the large amounts of alcohol they had consumed.

Expecting further punishment for their disgraceful actions, they begged for mercy, blaming the alcohol and each other for their uncharacteristic behaviour. Zhonghong, being the forgiving former monk that he was, let the boys go, providing they promised to never come back to Yongchun. This they did wholeheartedly.

However, what little pride they might have had was severely bruised at the embarrassment of being beaten by a much older man. So when they were at a safe distance from Zhonghong's house, one of the cowards turned around and shouted, "You old fool. You shouldn't have let us go. Mark my words, we'll get you back for this, I promise you!"

Zhonghong turned sharply back towards them, and like scared little rabbits, they ran as fast as they could back to their own village.

After the terrible events of that day, Zhonghong Fang vowed to himself that he would ensure the safety of his wife and daughter and keep his promise to Qiniang. The very next day he began passing on all of his skill and knowledge of Eighteen Monk Fist Boxing to them both.

After very little tuition indeed, it became clear that Qiniang had a natural talent for the fighting arts. Surely no father in the whole world could have been more proud of his daughter than Zhonghong was of Qiniang. He was sure that with several more months of training, Qiniang would be able to adequately defend herself and, furthermore, he was sure that one day she would become a great Master like him.

14
Qiniang's World Is Shattered

Sadly, Zhonghong would never see his daughter grow into the great martial artist that she was destined to be. On one particularly dark and stormy night, the three drunken ruffians returned to Yongchun bent on revenge. With the driving rain and crashing thunder drowning out any noise they might have made, and the black clouds casting a veil over the moon and stars, they crept like sewer rats in the darkness into the Fang family home.

Skulking from room to room, they searched the house until they found Zhonghong and his wife sleeping peacefully in their bedroom. For a few moments they stood over the peacefully oblivious couple, sniggering to each other as the lightening illuminated their evil, grinning faces. The perverse excitement of their nocturnal invasion and the foul crime they were about to commit sent adrenalin coursing through their veins.

Then, like a starter pistol, a blinding flash of lightening and an almighty crash of thunder jolted the intruders into action. Their faces were twisted and contorted like medieval gargoyles as they unleashed a ruthless, unrelenting, and cowardly attack on the kindly and wise Zhonghong and his wife. In the next room, lost in a deep and peaceful slumber, their beloved daughter never heard a sound.

Qiniang awoke to a bright, fresh, beautiful day, and a wide sunny smile spread across her face at the thought of another martial arts lesson with her beloved father. She threw off the blanket and got dressed as quick as a flash. Pulling back the screen door, she started towards her parents' room to wake them, so keen was she to get on with her training. As she reached the bedroom door her world was suddenly shattered by the heart-wrenching sound of her mother wailing uncontrollably and crying out, "No, no, no!"

Qiniang's heart began racing and pounding in her chest. As she reached for the door, her hand trembled at the thought of what she might find on the other side of it. After a momentary pause, she tore back the screen door and dropped to her knees, as all her strength was ripped from her body at the horrific sight before her.

Her mother, though terribly beaten, had survived the attack, but her father, the great Zhonghong Fang, his face unrecognizable from the barrage of blows he had received, lay limp and lifeless in his distraught wife's arms.

Qiniang knelt and stared with glazed and disbelieving eyes, but she did not cry; she could not cry. Although deeply heartbroken, it was another emotion that she felt filling every fibre of her body. Anger! All-consuming, raging, powerful anger accompanied by an overwhelming desire for revenge upon the evil beasts that had killed her father and destroyed her family.

15
Qiniang and the White Cranes

With her heartbroken mother's help, Qiniang continued her training every day, the rage and goal of revenge fuelling her every effort. She practised and practised as hard as she possibly could, hour upon hour, day upon day, and week upon week. Despite her very best efforts, though, her father's untimely death had robbed her not only of his love and affection but also of his complete knowledge and guidance in the way of Monk Fist Boxing.

Then something happened that changed the course of Qiniang's training and consequently her life. She had been working for hours trying to remember and perfect a technique that her father had shown her called 'Twin Dragons Playing with a Pearl', but was getting nowhere fast. She tried and tried and tried and tried again, but to no avail.

Quite suddenly, in a fit of shear frustration, all of the grief, sadness, and bottled-up anger that filled her erupted like molten magma from a volcano. She collapsed screaming and sobbing to the dusty ground, where she lay for what seemed like an eternity, crying and beating the ground with her bare fists. She had shed so many tears that small pools of mud formed where they fell.

Just as her anger and frustration were waning and she began to regain her composure, an almighty racket erupted from within a nearby bamboo grove. Qiniang, her curiosity aroused, wiped away her tears and picked herself up. As quietly and carefully as she could, she pushed her way through the bamboo grove. As she approached a clearing in the grove, she parted the tall green stalks to reveal the source of the commotion. There in the clearing were two magnificent white cranes, which appeared to be having a confrontation over territory.

Never taking their piercing yellow eyes off each other, the huge birds ferociously attacked one another with their razor-sharp beaks, feet, and huge wings. The young girl noticed how each was able to avoid the other with amazing speed and precision. Qiniang sat hypnotized, observing the intricacies of the fight for several minutes. Then, fearing that these beautiful birds may kill each other, Qiniang decided it might be best to try and separate them by chasing them off.

She grabbed a length of bamboo and started to make swinging and stabbing motions towards one and then the other. The birds made absolutely no attempt to fly away and just skipped, ducked, and dodged all of her efforts at moving them on. If Qiniang hadn't known better, she might have thought that they were enjoying making a fool of her. She was sure that the birds only flew their separate ways when they had grown sufficiently bored of teasing her.

Absolutely exhausted from her efforts, Qiniang made her way home, but she could not stop thinking about the white cranes and how they fought. Recalling them in her mind's eye, she studied their fast, elusive attacks and graceful, evasive, defensive movements. If she could somehow move as the white cranes had, she would be an invincible fighter.

For three years, Qiniang continued to practise the art of Monk Fist Boxing that her father had shown her, but she also developed incredibly elusive movements based on what she had learned from watching the cranes. By combining her father's art with her own white crane techniques, she became a great Master of her own style of fighting, which became known as Yongchun White Crane Boxing.

Her reputation as an invincible fighter spread far and wide to every corner of China and beyond. Many men challenged her to matches, as their arrogance did not allow them to believe that they could be beaten by a mere woman. Qiniang met every challenge and never, ever lost a match. She gained the respect of many of her challengers, who then became her disciples and students.

Now that she finally had amazing fighting skills, experience, and a growing reputation, she found that she no longer needed to exact revenge upon the men that had murdered her father. All of her anger had been expelled from her the day she first encountered the white cranes fighting.

Through her training she had discovered the confidence, calmness, and an inner peace that had been stripped from her when her father's life was cruelly taken. She knew that Zhonghong, being a kind and peaceful Shaolin monk, would never have wanted her to resort to violence. She also knew that he would be extremely proud of her now.

16
The Importance of Qiniang Fang

Chinese merchants and dignitaries regularly made the journey to Okinawa from the area around Qiniang's village. They took with them their knowledge of the Chinese fighting arts, especially White Crane Boxing. White Crane Boxing was then blended with the Okinawan fighting styles, and it was this blending and exchange of ideas that would one day play a huge part in the creation of Karate-Do.

Qiniang also taught that her fighting style was only ever to be used to defend oneself, loved ones, or those unable to defend themselves. This also became one of the core philosophies of Karate.

17
Satunushi 'Toda' Sakugawa—The Petulant Youth

China had strong trade links, partly governed, and therefore had a great cultural influence over Okinawa for many centuries. For this reason, Chinese merchants and dignitaries were regular visitors to the tiny island, bringing with them their literature, traditions, and, of course, their fighting arts. One such man, Kusankun, was a master of Qiniang Fang's White Crane Boxing.

On one particularly hot and humid day in Shuri, the royal capital of Okinawa, Kusankun was taking a stroll along a country lane which had a stream running alongside it. Ahead of him he noticed a group of young men who were looking his way, whispering, and giggling amongst themselves.

As he approached them, he stopped and bowed respectfully, just as we would stop and politely say good morning to someone. As he bowed, one of the youths cruelly pushed him into the stream, where he landed in a most undignified manner, soaking his fine silk clothes.

Bursting into hysterical laughter, the unruly gang pointed and jeered at the sodden Kusankun sitting in the stream. The young man who had pushed him, the tallest of the gang, stood defiantly staring at Kusankun with his arms crossed while his cronies patted his back in congratulation.

Kusankun, appearing completely unbothered, looked directly toward his arrogant attacker, smiled, and cheerily said, "Thank you, young man," whilst holding out his hand to the petulant youth as if expecting him to help him out of the water.

The calm attitude of Kusankun caught the group unawares, and their laughter quickly subsided into an uneasy silence. The first to speak was the tall, defiant youth, who barked angrily, "Thank you! What do you mean thank you, you crazy Chinaman?" He was obviously disappointed at not riling his victim.

"Well, with the day being so very hot, I was just thinking of taking a dip in this cool stream. Although I did not intend to do it fully clothed, it is still most refreshing, so thank you. Now help me up, there's a good lad," replied Kusankun, still reaching out his hand for assistance.

The bemused youth maintained a calm exterior but inside, his blood was beginning to boil. Straining a smile at the soaking stranger, in a very sarcastic tone of voice he responded, "Always glad to be of assistance, sir," and then held out his hand to help Kusankun up with the full intention of pushing him straight back in.

Kusankun took the youth's hand, and before he knew what was happening, the expert fighter's other hand immediately gripped his lapel.

Pulling the surprised youth to him so that their noses were almost touching, Kusankun cheekily smiled and said, "Now please allow me to return the favour, sir."

With lightening speed, he turned and threw the bemused boy over his shoulder and into the shallow stream, where he landed painfully on his back.

The enraged youth, who, as it turned out, was quite a skilled fighter, got to his feet and threw a flurry of angry attacks at Kusankun. No matter how he tried, he could not even get close to this impudent tourist. He seemed to him like a ghost, for it was as if he were grabbing and lunging at thin air. Realizing he had well and truly met his match, the embarrassed and humbled youngster conceded defeat.

"What is your name, boy?" Kusankun asked.

The boy straightened up and proudly replied, "I am Satunushi Sakugawa, sir," and bowed in respect to the better fighter.

Returning the bow, Kusankun said, "Well, Satunushi Sakugawa, I believe we have much to talk about."

18
'Tode'

Born in Shuri on Okinawa in the year 1733, Satunushi Sakugawa, just like Qiniang Fang, lost his father when he was very young at the hands of a group of drunken thugs. Before he died, Sakugawa's father made his son promise that he would learn how to defend himself and never to be a victim, as he had been.

Following his father's wishes, Sakugawa sought out a martial arts instructor, which was not as easy as you may think, as the fighting arts were highly secretive on Okinawa at this time. Eventually, after a lot of persuasion, he managed to find a great Master in the art of To-de willing to teach him. This great man's name was Takahara, a Buddhist monk and a member of the royal bodyguard.

Sakugawa studied under his elderly master for six years until Takahara grew too old and weak to continue his lessons. Just before he died, Takahara asked Sakugawa to take the name 'Tode' in honour of him and his beloved art. Sakugawa was extremely proud to do this for his Master and has been remembered throughout history as 'Tode' Sakugawa.

19
A New Teacher

Following their introduction to one another at the stream, Kusankun and Sakugawa talked for a little while of Chinese and Okinawan fighting systems. Kusankun decided that he liked the boy's spirit and that his petulant ways were probably due to losing his father at such a young age and having to fend for himself.

Patting the boy on the back, he said, "How would you like to learn my fighting system?"

Sakugawa was still in awe at the ease in which Kusankun had beaten him and immediately accepted the offer, eager to learn the Chinese man's superior skills. So it was that with a firm, manly handshake, Kusankun became Sakugawa's new master and mentor.

"Meet me tonight after sunset at this very spot," Kusankun ordered and began to walk away.

Sakugawa called after him, "But, Master Kusankun, there is no light here after dark and the nights on these country lanes are as black as pitch!"

Without even turning around, Kusankun shouted, "Perfect!" and went on his way, leaving a slightly confused Sakugawa behind him scratching his head and wondering how on earth they would be able to practise in the dark.

20
A Lesson in Night Fighting

It was a nervous and excited Sakugawa that made his way to meet his new teacher that evening. Kusankun, feeling the boy's apprehension, explained that the most dangerous time of the day is when darkness falls. It is then that the dregs of society, such as muggers, thieves, and drunken thugs, wander through the dark streets preying on unsuspecting and ill-prepared victims.

"A man who can easily defend himself when blinded by the darkness need not fear anyone," he said.

He led Sakugawa by flaming torchlight to a particularly dark area of woodland next to the stream where they'd had their first fateful meeting. Kusankun then tossed the torch into the stream to extinguish it and they were both immediately shrouded in darkness.

"Let us begin!" Kusankun called to the boy, followed by, "Come on and strike me if you can!"

"But I cannot see you now the torch is out!" Sakugawa replied. "How can I hit what I cannot see?"

He received a firm push in the back and Kusankun repeated the order: "Strike me!" Then from the side: "Strike me!" Then from in front again: "Strike me! Strike me! Ha-ha!" the wily Chinaman merrily taunted his young protégé. "Come on, boy. What's wrong with you? Strike me!"

Just as on the previous day, the poor, helpless Sakugawa felt that he was fighting a ghost. His arms and feet punched, kicked, and flailed around, hitting nothing but the cool, fresh Okinawan night air. Finally, frustrated and embarrassed, he refused to play Kusankun's game any longer. "I did not come here to be made a fool of. It is impossible to see or strike anything in this darkness," he angrily shouted. Then he stood with his arms crossed and his chin resting on his chest in a child-like sulk.

Quite suddenly, a firm hand gripped his shoulder from the front and spun him round, and in an instant he felt an arm encircle his neck and begin to strangle him. As much he struggled he could not get out of the vice-like grip. His last thoughts before he finally succumbed to unconsciousness were, 'This is it. I am going to die just for pushing a crazy Chinaman into a stream.' Then everything went black.

21
What a Relief

A warm fire, the smell of burning pine mixed with that of fresh tea, and a grinning Kusankun greeted Tode as he slowly regained consciousness.

"I am not dead?" Relief overwhelmed him.

"No, you are perfectly fine," Kusankun replied. "You have just finished your first lesson."

"Which was what? Never trust a Chinaman?" Sakugawa asked in good humour.

"Perhaps so." Kusankun's grin broadened. "Now listen to me, Tode. If you cannot see your opponent, you must be silent and allow your remaining senses of smell, hearing, and touch to compensate."

"What do you mean, Master Kusankun?"

Kusankun went on. "In darkness, an enemy that you cannot see, you may be able to hear or even smell, especially if he hasn't washed in a little while, or has been drinking liquor. These things will betray him and give away his position. Once located, you can touch him; once you can touch him you can hold and control him; once you can control him you can defeat him, as I defeated you…again!"

For another six years, Tode was mentored by the great Kusankun and always in the darkness of night. So that he could better remember the techniques, Tode created a kata and named it 'Kusanku' in honour of his Chinese Master. This kata was to become one of the cornerstones of modern Karate and is still practised today as Kushanku or Kanku.

Tode's skills at night fighting became equal to, and maybe even surpassed, those of his great Master Kusankun, which was just as well, as they would soon be put to the sternest of tests.

22
Tode's's Pirate Adventure

Tode's fighting skills soon became legendary throughout Okinawa, and due to his association with Takagawa, he became a bodyguard to the royal family. Okinawa was partly governed by China, so every year the royal family had to send what was called a 'Tribute Ship' filled with valuable cargo to the Chinese mainland in honour of the Emperor.

Tode Sakugawa was ordered to sail with the tribute vessel to protect its cargo and the returning Chinese dignitaries on board. He found this great responsibility extremely exciting, as it provided him with an opportunity to learn even more about Chinese culture, especially their fighting arts, during his visit.

Tode stood proudly upon the bow of the ship as it set sail on the most glorious morning he could ever recall. The sun was rising over Okinawa, the breeze was perfect for sailing, and everyone aboard was in fine fettle and going about their duties with gusto.

To pass the time during the long journey, Tode spent hours practising his precious Kushanku kata on the deck. The sailors found this most amusing and would take great pleasure in mimicking and poking fun at him. Tode, completely focused on his training, would simply ignore them or shoot them a piercing glare that would send them back to their duties in an instant.

As the sun set in the west on that first day's sailing, Tode checked that everything was satisfactory for the dignitaries in his care. He then returned to the bow of the ship where he could relax and gaze at the stars. The breeze that had carried them along so well during the day was now as light as a sleeping baby's breath. The ship was barely moving, and gently swayed and bobbed on a sea that was as calm and still as a garden pond.

All seemed well, but behind them, hidden on the horizon in a thick bank of fog, mortal danger loomed in the form of a Chinese pirate ship. Under full sail and with the benefit of a stiff breeze, the pirates were steadily, mile by mile, catching up with Tode's tribute ship.

As the night air cooled, the fog caught up and consumed Tode's ship, making it impossible to see more than a few feet in any direction. Sailors at this time had to use the stars to navigate, but as the swirling fog now obscured them, they could not be sure of their direction. The sails were lowered, the anchor dropped, and lanterns hung at the bow and stern of the ship so that some onboard duties could continue.

For the pirates, the fog was the perfect cover, and now the lantern lights betrayed the tribute ship's position, acting as stars, guiding them directly to their quarry. Before very long they had caught up with the anchored ship. As they approached, the pirates lowered their sails, and as silently as a feather on the breeze, they glided in alongside the surely doomed vessel.

Onboard Tode's China-bound vessel all was quiet, and many of the crew and passengers were relaxing below deck. Those above deck had also been lulled into a state of drowsiness by boredom and the gentle rocking motion of the ship. All, that is, except for Tode, whose senses, fine-tuned over six years' night training with Kusankun, were telling him something was seriously wrong.

He was fully alert when the pirate ship drifted in, and having seen it he immediately put out the bow lantern. He now crept his away stealthily along the ship to extinguish the stern lantern whilst quietly alerting the men up on deck to their predicament as he went. As he reached the stern lantern and blew out the flame, a fearsome 'kiai' (spirit breath/shout) from the pirates cut through the fog like a samurai sword through flesh and bone, and all hell broke loose!

There was no time to alert the men below decks as he had intended. Tode had to do something now! The pirates poured onboard, ten, fifteen, maybe twenty of them, instilling dread and fear among the peaceful sailors with their deafening roars. Ferocious hand-to-hand battles were taking place all over the ship, with the warrior pirates soon gaining the upper hand.

Ruthlessly, they began throwing the cut and bloodied sailors overboard with the full intention of leaving them to drown or be devoured by sharks. The pirates meant to get away with the entire tribute ship and its valuable cargo intact.

Utilizing his training, Tode began making his way around the ship in the darkness, picking off the pirates one by one. Using the grabbing, throwing, and strangling techniques, which were now second nature to him, he began to dispatch the pirates to the sea with efficiency and surprising ease.

Confusion and doubt began to spread amongst the marauding interlopers as they noticed their numbers quickly depleting. Being the superstitious sort that pirates often were, some of them threw themselves overboard, believing that a spirit, demon, or even the gods themselves were protecting this cursed ship!

With the crew from below decks reinforcing Tode's amazingly elusive efforts, the pirates were eventually outnumbered and finally defeated. Thanks to Sakugawa, not one of the tribute ship's crew was lost in the attempted hijacking, and from that day on not one of the tribute ship's crew made fun of their new hero, Tode Sakugawa, when he practised his Kushanku kata up on deck.

23
The Importance of Tode Sakugawa

During his lifetime, Sakugawa travelled to China and the Shaolin Monastery many times, and returned to Okinawa with knowledge of new kata and fighting techniques, which are still practised by karateka all around the world to this day. His own Kushanku or Kanku kata, which he created in honour of his great Master, was to become the cornerstone of modern Karate.

Many of the techniques and combinations from Kushanku were taken and used by Yasutsune Itosu to create the 'Pinan' or 'Heian' group of kata. These kata are fundamentally important to many styles of Karate that are practised today. When you begin your Karate training, these are often the very first forms you learn.

Tode Sakugawa ensured his legacy and guaranteed the future of Karate-Do by delivering his incredible knowledge of the fighting arts into the hands of another very important link in the chain of great Karate Masters.

Satunushi 'Tode' Sakugawa died on 17th August 1815 at the grand old age of eighty-two.

24
Sokon 'Bushi' Matsumura—Matsumura and Tode

Tode Sakugawa was nearly eighty years old when a rather rough and ready fourteen-year-old boy approached him and asked if the great Master would teach him how to fight. The cocky youth explained that although he was already a superior martial artist, he had ambitions to become the best fighter in the whole of Okinawa. Tode really didn't want to take on a new student at his age, and knowing the lad and his reputation for being a bully and a troublemaker, flatly refused.

Determined to have Tode for his teacher, the persistent lad sent his father to speak to the elderly Master. He stood silently and respectfully as his father pleaded with Tode to allow his son to become his disciple, promising that he would work very hard and never disappoint the venerable Master should he choose to mentor him.

Turning to face Master Tode with a respectful bow and a twinkle in his eye, the teenager, who could be extremely charming when required, decided that it was time for him to speak for himself. "Honourable Master, please accept my apologies for the arrogance I displayed when I first approached you. If you honour me with your time and infinite knowledge, I promise to empty my mind of all that I think I know, so that it can be filled with everything that you undoubtedly know. I assure you that I will never give you reason to question my loyalty should you agree to become my teacher. Furthermore, I will do my utmost to make you very proud of me."

The eloquent and respectful delivery had the desired effect. As the boy reminded Tode of himself when he was a rather petulant youth, he agreed to take him on as his protégé on one condition: "Know this! I give no second chances. Disobey or disregard any of my instructions in any way and I will consider this arrangement finished." Master Tode then ordered both the boy and his father to go, as he required an afternoon nap. As the boy and his father were about to leave, Master Tode added, "It is not a requirement that you should make me proud of you. You should endeavour always to be proud of yourself." With a tired wave of his hand, he dismissed them.

The very fortunate young man, who had just acquired the tutelage of one of greatest Karate Masters in all of history, was Sokon 'Bushi' Matsumura.

25
Sokon 'Bushi' Matsumura—Royal Protector

Matsumura was born around 1800. Even as a child he was completely obsessed with the martial arts. By the time he became Tode Sakugawa's student at the age of fourteen, he had already gained a reputation as a very skilled fighter. He had also earned the unfortunate reputation for being rather hotheaded and a bit of a troublemaker.

Benefiting from Tode's incredible knowledge and wisdom, Matsumura developed into the most revered and fearsome martial artist in all Okinawa. His incredible speed and power soon became legendary and his style of Karate became known as Shuri-te after his hometown and the royal capital of Okinawa, Shuri.

Sadly, after only a few years' training, the great Master Tode Sakugawa died at the unusually old age of eighty-two. Matsumura was deeply saddened at this loss and promised himself that his Master and friend Tode would never be forgotten and that his wisdom would live on through him.

Matsumura's reputation was so revered in Shuri that he was employed as a bodyguard to the Okinawan king at just twenty years old. Before he reached thirty years old, he became the Chief Bodyguard to the royal family of Okinawa, which at his young age was unheard of.

26
If Looks Could Kill

Matsumura was unusual amongst Okinawan men of that time in that he was quite tall and had what are often described as 'very unusual, piercing, hawk-like eyes'. It was said that he could defeat any man with just a glare and that his eyes could cut through an opponent's resolve as easily as a samurai sword could cut through flesh.

On one particular occasion whilst in a particularly foul mood, Matsumura barged into the shop of a local engraver with the intention of getting his tobacco pipe engraved. His unfortunate temper getting the better of him, he spoke quite rudely to the craftsman. The engraver was also a renowned martial artist, and though much older than Matsumura, was a fit, powerful bull of a man.

"Aren't you the King's bodyguard and Karate instructor, Master Matsumura?" he asked, already knowing perfectly well that he was.

"No, I am not. Not any more, and in fact I wish I'd never heard of Karate or that arrogant ass of a King!" was the bad-tempered reply.

This response shocked the engraver, as he knew that Matsumura had always been fanatical about his Karate. Curious about what was troubling the angry young man, he offered him tea and his ear, telling him, "You may speak to me and empty your mind of all its troubles."

Matsumura proceeded, in between taking sips of the very good tea, to rant on about what a poor Karate student the King was. "He is annoyingly impatient and does not want to learn the basic techniques first. He insists on surging ahead with advanced moves beyond, it must be said, his very poor ability."

"Then why did you not refuse to teach him, Master Matsumura," enquired the engraver.

"Refuse! Refuse! How could I refuse? For one thing he was my employer and for another he is the King!" replied an incredulous Matsumura.

"Did I hear you mention that he *was* your employer?" asked the engraver.

"Yes, you did," answered Matsumura. He then explained that during kumite, or fighting practice, the King had attempted to open an attack on him with a nidan geri (double kick). "A nidan geri! Against me! A nidan geri!" Matsumura's astonishment was plainly clear to see, and once again he began to lose his temper. Then he continued to tell the engraver how insulted he had been that someone of the King's fighting ineptitude would have the audacity to try such a ridiculous technique on the likes of him.

Rather than let the King win, as most would have done to protect their position within the royal court, the belligerent bodyguard thought he would teach his royal student a valuable lesson. Matsumura blocked the kick and then crashed himself into the King with all his strength, sending him sprawling on the floor. His royal employer had been very badly battered and bruised, and in a fierce rage, dismissed Matsumura from the palace until further notice.

"And that was over one hundred days ago! I've heard nothing of the King since and I hope I never do." Outburst over, Matsumura drew a deep breath and took another sip of the tea.

"Oh my, that is bad luck," the engraver sympathized. Then he said, "Well, if you're no longer the King's teacher, why don't you teach me instead?"

Matsumura tilted his head toward the engraver and suspiciously frowned. "You are known in Naha and Shuri as a great fighter in your own right. Why would a man such as you require further instruction?" he queried.

"To receive tuition from the King's own instructor would greatly enhance my reputation as a martial artist, and to be frank, I would also like to see just how good you really are."

The engraver's tone of voice had now changed, and he appeared, Matsumura thought, to be trying to goad him. This re-ignited Matsumura's short fuse and he exploded like a bomb. "I have no intention of teaching Karate to anyone ever again. Ever! Do you hear me? What is more, I certainly do not need or have the inclination to prove myself to the likes of you." Slamming his empty teacup down with such fury that it shattered into pieces, Matsumura launched himself to his feet and charged towards the exit.

"You refuse to teach me, but would you also refuse to fight me?" the craftsman retorted before Matsumura had time to leave.

Matsumura stopped dead in his tracks, took another deep breath, and slowly turned to face the audacious artisan. "I don't believe I just heard you correctly, sir," the ever so slightly shocked Matsumura calmly replied. "You dare to challenge me to a match? Knowing who I am, you would be so ridiculously dim as to challenge me to a match?"

"Your hearing is perfectly fine, Matsumura. I did indeed challenge you to a match. Do you accept my challenge, or are all the stories I've heard about you just that, stories?" The engraver's tone of voice and choice of words had now lost all sign of respect for his guest.

Calmness had now descended over the previously outraged, former royal bodyguard as he replied with some irony and much truth, "Very well, sir, I accept your challenge. You decide the time and place and I will certainly oblige by making your death wish a reality, for I believe you have bitten off far more than even a man of your rotund stature can chew."

Having achieved exactly what he had intended from the moment Matsumura had entered his shop, the grinning engraver ignored the taller man's sarcasm and announced, "Five o'clock tomorrow morning in the graveyard. We shall see who has bitten off more than he can chew."

You must realize that such a challenge in the time of Matsumura was not just about protecting one's honour but also a serious matter of life and death, as these duals could be fatal for one or both participants. So the chain of events that the engraver had just set in motion were, to say the least, extremely serious indeed.

At five o'clock sharp the following morning, the men stood facing each other about four meters apart. Respectfully bowing to each other, as tradition requires, the engraver immediately dropped into a Karate stance ready to attack. Rather peculiarly, Matsumura, on the other hand, just stood there nonchalantly with his arms crossed and his head lolling to one side, almost as if dozing.

The engraver decided to take advantage of Matsumura's odd behaviour and, surprisingly quickly for a man of his size, he advanced towards his opponent. As he got within a metre or so and was about to launch his first attack, Matsumura's head snapped up and his terrifying, hawk-like eyes burned straight into the eyes of his opponent. The engraver halted in his tracks, his legs turned to jelly, his heart began to race, and sweat began to pour from his brow. In confusion, he retreated to a nearby rock, where he sat trying to recover from this most unusual reaction.

He was brought to his senses by Matsumura calling to him, "Come on, man. I haven't got all day. Let's get on with it!"

Taking a deep breath to settle his sudden onset of nerves, the older man shakily got to his feet and began to advance again. Matsumura just stood in the same relaxed position as if he didn't have a care in the world. With a mighty roar that would put a lion to shame, the older man launched another attack.

Once again, Matsumura, who was completely unnerved, directed another piercing glare at the advancing man. It was as if an invisible wall had sprung up in front of the engraver, as the energy exuding from Matsumura's terrifying stare sapped all his strength and he collapsed.

Matsumura smiled and called to his opponent, "You can't beat anyone by merely shouting and sitting down. Why don't you attack me properly?"

Realizing he had no chance of victory, the engraver decided that he would put everything into this, his last attack, even though it could very well mean certain death. Rising to his feet, he composed himself as best he could. At that exact moment, Matsumura unleashed a deafening, guttural kiai that hammered into his now terrified opponent's chest like a spectral sledgehammer. Stunned to a halt, the engraver shot a disbelieving glance at this mighty warrior, only to be hit once again by the invisible lightning bolts of energy that shot from those mystical and terrifying eyes.

His own eyes now as wide as saucers from fear, the engraver found that he could not move even an inch and again collapsed, a quivering, confused, pleading wreck of a man. "Please, Master Matsumura, no more, no more. I concede to your superiority. I was a fool to ever challenge you."

Matsumura, taking pity on his vanquished opponent, walked over to him and helped him to his feet. Whilst the engraver brushed down his dust-covered clothing with hands that he could barely control, Matsumura told him that his spirit and bravery were as mighty as any martial artist he had ever met. "You showed a warrior's courage when you continued to at least try and attack, even though you knew you were defeated." Matsumura comforted.

For the rest of his life, the engraver told tales of his encounter with the great Matsumura and the very high regard with which he held him.

Just days after the match, Matsumura was recalled to Shuri Castle, where he went on to serve as a loyal bodyguard to three consecutive Okinawan kings in a career lasting fifty years.

27
Bushi the Bullfighter

When Matsumura was a young man, Okinawa was jointly ruled by China from afar, and more directly by the ruthless Satsuma samurai warrior clan from Kyushu in Japan. They had invaded Okinawa in 1609, and the highly trained and experienced warriors swiftly crushed the helpless Uchinanchu (Okinawan people) in battle.

As you are already aware, Okinawa did have a king and a royal court. However, they had no real power and were just the puppets of their Satsuma overlords, who used them to appease the Okinawan people. The first king that Matsumura served as a bodyguard, and the same king that felt Matsumura's wrath in the previous story, was King Sho Ko. He was reputedly quite mad and not a reliable figurehead for the Satsuma samurai, so they decided that it would be best if they 'retired' him.

The King, having received the news of his enforced abdication, decided that he would hold a great event to celebrate, as he saw it, his memorable reign. On the spur of the moment and with very little thought at all, he announced to all Okinawa that his best bodyguard, Matsumura, was to fight a bull to the death using only his bare hands!

As you can imagine, this was incredibly exciting news for the Uchinanchu. A man fighting a bull! Such a thing had never been seen or heard of before. The only person so far unaware of this spectacularly dangerous event was the one man who should have been informed first, Matsumura himself. He had been on a visit to China when the announcement was made and was completely oblivious to the demented King's debacle of an idea.

The first he heard of it was whilst wandering through the market in Shuri. He overheard a merchant talking to a customer about how good the event would be for business, as hoards of people would flock into Shuri from all over Okinawa.

"What event do you speak of?" Matsumura inquired. As Chief of Security to the royal family, he was supposed to be kept informed of everything happening on the island.

The merchant, immediately recognizing Matsumura, replied, "Why, your event, honourable sir. Your great fight."

Matsumura, obviously, did not understand. "My great fight! What do you mean my great fight, and with whom is this fight to be?"

"With whom, sir?" The merchant sounded surprised. "Surely you mean with what?" Now everyone was getting confused.

Matsumura, becoming agitated, blurted out, "That's quite enough of this jabbering. Just tell me I'm supposed to be fighting and when!"

The bemused and nervous merchant replied, "You are to fight a bull with your bare hands a week from tomorrow, for the King's celebration."

Matsumura closed his eyes, shook his head, and let out a long, resigned sigh. 'Oh no!' he thought. 'What has that mad monarch gone and got me into now?'

Matsumura was a proud man and he knew that he would never be able to show his face on the streets of Shuri again if he refused to fight the animal. He had to think of a way to defeat the bull without getting himself killed, and think of it quickly. Spotting an item on a shelf behind the merchant, a smile slowly spread across his face. The merchant and his customer looked at each other and then back to Matsumura.

"Are you feeling all right, Master Matsumura?" the customer enquired.

Still smiling, Matsumura turned to the merchant again and asked, "My good man, would you be so kind as to sell me one of those ladies' hairpins you have there, please?"

"Yes, sir, of course," he replied in a tone betraying his curiosity, and handed the still smiling Matsumura the requested item. Matsumura paid the man and turned to leave. "A gift for your lovely wife?" the prying merchant called after him.

"No, it's for me," replied Matsumura, and off he went, marching at double time.

The merchant and his customer once again looked at each other and shrugged their shoulders in intrigue. What would a man want with a lady's hairpin?

Matsumura had struck upon an idea that just might save him from a very grisly death. Every day for the rest of the week before the fight, he secretly visited his long-horned opponent in its stall. Grabbing the bull's nose-ring, he would stare at the animal with his terrifying eyes and then stab the poor beast sharply in the nose with the hairpin. If you are wondering how this seemingly cruel behaviour would help Matsumura defeat the animal in a fight, then please read on.

The day of the great event arrived, and hundreds of people from all over the island descended upon Shuri Castle. Most were sure that the fight would be concluded very quickly and in the bull's favour. The local bookkeepers were inundated with bets from people looking to make some easy money. As you might have guessed, the vast majority of the bets were on the bull to win.

The Master of Ceremonies made his way into the centre of the arena and the crowd fell silent. "Ladies and gentleman, in honour of our most esteemed highness, King Sho Ko of Okinawa, I am proud to introduce to you the bravest, most fearsome and…" 'Soon to be deceased', he thought to himself. "…man in the whole of Okinawa, MAT-SU-MUURRRRAAAA!"

A cacophony of cheering, shouting, and applause erupted as Matsumura confidently marched into the arena. Making his way to the centre of the fighting area, he prepared himself for this momentous battle.

The crowd once again fell silent in anticipation of the bull's arrival. Somewhere in the background it could be heard snorting, pawing, and stamping on the ground as it was tormented into a terrible rage.

Then at one end of the arena, the crowd began to stir and move aside. The bull was coming! Matsumura appeared completely cool, in fact almost bored, as he turned ready to face his destiny. Then a murmur spread like ripples on a pond through the mesmerized audience. The murmur became a shout, the shout became cheering and then, as the beast burst into the arena, the cheering became an almighty roar of excitement!

This was it. Battle would commence, and surely this poor man would die an extremely grizzly but honourable death, sent to the afterlife by a bull's horns and a king's madness. Then, as quickly as they had erupted into a frenzied, baying, bloodthirsty mob, the crowd was reduced to a stunned, disbelieving silence.

The bull, having charged into the arena, had come face to face with Matsumura, who just stood stock-still and stared at the massive hulk of a beast without flinching. The shocked animal had immediately recognized those dreadful eyes that had been terrorizing it for whole week and had ground to a halt. Expecting to be stabbed in the nose with Matsumura's hairpin, it backed away, turned around, and scrambled from the arena in a rather more timid fashion than it had entered!

A single voice from somewhere in the audience shouted Matsumura's name. Then the entire audience joined in as one, with a great chant of, "Matsumura! Matsumura! Matsumura!" Okinawa had found a new hero.

The King was so proud of his bodyguard that he gave him the new name of 'Bushi', which means warrior. His reputation as a legendary martial artist secured, Matsumura went on to be bodyguard for two more Okinawan kings, who, by the way, were not in the slightest bit mad.

28
Matsumura and Chinto

Okinawa has been called the 'Island of Typhoons', as it is battered by the powerful tropical storms on a regular basis. It was due to a particularly terrible typhoon that Matsumura met a sailor who was to have a massive influence on his Karate.

The typhoon winds were so strong that trees were being bent to the very point of snapping. Barrows, buckets, and any other item not fixed down were being carried away down the muddied and deserted Okinawan streets. Fortunately for the islanders, their homes were built low and strong, providing shelter and safety from this, the worst typhoon in living memory.

Others, however, were not so fortunate. Way out at sea, the crew of a Chinese merchant ship bound for Japan was being tossed around like vegetables in a wok by the mountainous waves. The ship's sails had been torn from the mast and many of the crew had already been lost to the boiling seas. Now miles off course and heading towards jagged and treacherous rocks, the lives of the remaining crewmen were in the hands of the gods.

As they approached the rocks, a shipwreck seemed certain, but a sudden swell of the sea lifted the vessel. For a brief and wonderful moment it seemed like the surge would miraculously carry the ship safely over the patiently waiting jagged and hungry stone teeth. The men held their breath and braced themselves, and some even dared to smile at what seemed to be their lucky escape. Then the black sky got impossibly darker and a look of absolute terror appeared on the face of one sailor as he pointed upwards, seemingly towards the sky.

His comrades followed his terrified stare and, to their horror, realized that it was not the sky that he was pointing to. There, rising high above the ship's main mast, was a gargantuan wave. As they watched, it seemed to pause above them as if giving them a moment to say a final prayer before the inevitable. Then, with incredible force, it crashed down on top of the ship, smashing it to pieces on the rocks below. Against all the odds, one very fit, strong, and incredibly lucky sailor somehow survived the freak wave and managed to reach shore near Naha on Okinawa. That sailor's name was Chinto.

Shipwrecked in a foreign land with no friends, Chinto now had to try to somehow survive until he could stow away on a boat back to China. Rather than seek the help of the local people, Chinto stayed alive by stealing food from their stores and clothes from their washing lines. Eventually, his criminal activities became such a nuisance to the locals that word of the mysterious thief reached the King, who immediately ordered his best man, Bushi Matsumura, to capture him.

Chinto had been operating in and around the same area of Naha and Shuri since he had arrived there, so Matsumura decided to lay a trap for this elusive man. He had a local farmer's wife hang out her husband's washing and bake some fresh bread, hoping the irresistible smell would lure the starving sailor. Matsumura believed capturing a common thief would be a very simple task for a man of his superior ability, so decided not to bring any reinforcements and claim the glory for himself.

With the trap set, Bushi had the farmer's wife make him some tea and then hid behind the pigsty, which had the best vantage point. The sun set and by early evening it was quite dark, except for the lantern light coming from the farmhouse window. With his senses enhanced by four years of night training with Tode Sakugawa, Bushi was confident of beating anyone in these dark conditions, especially an untrained, good-for-nothing, ragamuffin thief.

The night drew on, becoming darker and colder, but Matsumura was a patient man and did not waver from his task. It was the early hours of the morning when CRACK! A twig snapped. Bushi, still fully alert, looked in the direction of the disturbance. The clothes hanging on the line to tempt the thief began to be removed. Quite amusingly, they appeared to move through the air on their own, as the thief could not be seen in the darkness, but Bushi was not smiling.

With the stealth of a panther, he began to silently stalk his way towards the bobbing movement of the clothing. Biding his time and choosing his moment wisely, he pounced, expecting to take down the thief. To his surprise, all he caught hold of was an armful of wet clothing being dangled on the end of a long pole by Chinto, who had anticipated a trap. Before he knew what was happening, Bushi was being grabbed from behind and thrown to the floor. This was not something the great Matsumura was at all used to, and he did not like it one bit!

"I have no desire to hurt you, but if you attempt to capture me, you will leave me with little choice. Please stay where you are and allow me to leave," Chinto warned the stunned Matsumura. He then ran off into the darkness, but did not get very far, as he promptly tripped over a bucket that was lying in the yard.

Bushi Matsumura, confounded and furious at this common thief's impudence, set off in the direction of the crash, only to find he was suddenly tumbling through the air as he fell over the prone sailor. Chinto was on the ground moaning and groaning as he gripped a very sore shin. Quickly regaining his senses, Matsumura scrambled along the ground and managed to get hold of Chinto's collar with his left hand. Pulling the sailor backwards to the floor, he managed to clamber his way on top of him and sat victoriously upon his chest.

"If anyone is going to get hurt here, it will be you, thief, so I suggest that you give yourself up quietly or you shall leave me with little choi— humphhh!" Bushi's victory speech was rudely interrupted by a hefty punch to his stomach, which knocked the wind clean out of his lungs. In a flash, Chinto bucked the breathless bodyguard over his head and onto the ground.

This was a new and shocking experience for Bushi, who had never been bettered in combat before. Consequently, he was determined it was not going to happen now. He climbed to his feet and listened for any sound or movement that would give away Chinto's position. There was the sound of running, a loud crack of wooden planks splitting, a cry of pain and the piercing squeals of pigs.

Matsumura chuckled as he realized that the unfortunate thief had run headlong into the pigsty! Bushi ran towards the squealing mayhem and dived onto the thief, who was now covered from head to toe in pig filth, the stench of which took both men's breath away and made their eyes stream with water.

The fight had been going on for so long now that the sun was beginning to rise in the eastern sky. Still engaged in a titanic battle, Matsumura suddenly became aware of the thief's ridiculously filthy appearance and, quite uncharacteristically, he began to laugh uncontrollably. Chinto, obviously seeing the joke and Matsumura's similar muck-covered appearance, also began to laugh hysterically. Both men collapsed to the floor overcome with fatigue and hysterics.

When Matsumura heard Chinto's sorry tale of the typhoon and the shipwreck, he took pity on the sailor. He offered to provide food and shelter for him until he could get back to China on the condition that he taught Matsumura his fighting system. Matsumura had never been matched by any man and wanted to be sure that it would never happen again.

Chinto agreed to Matsumura's terms and spent several months teaching his newfound friend his incredible martial art. Bushi recorded Chinto's system in a kata, which he named after the sailor. It is still practised today and is known as both Chinto and Gankaku, which means 'Crane on a Rock'.

29
The Importance of Matsumura

During his lifetime, Matsumura, like Sakugawa, often travelled to China and the Shaolin Monastery, returning with knowledge of new kata that are still at the core of Karate to this day, kata such as Gojoshiho, Naihanchi (tekki), and Seisan (hangetsu). As we have already discovered, he is responsible for Chinto kata (Gankaku), but he is also credited with creating Patsai or Bassai Dai kata. Bassai Dai is a landmark kata for any practising karateka, as it is regarded as the transition point from being a beginner to finally approaching the coveted black belt status.

Matsumura developed the hard and ruthless style of 'Shuri-te' Karate, instilling the philosophy of 'Ikken Hisatsu' or 'One attack, single death' into the men he trained. This hard, direct style of Karate-Do developed into several styles including Shotokan Karate.

Perhaps his greatest achievement, though, was ensuring the future development of Karate throughout the world by passing on his knowledge and expertise to the amazing men responsible for the global spread of the sporting phenomenon we know today.

30
Yasutsune 'Anko' Itosu the Powerhouse

Born in 1831 in Shuri, the royal capital of Okinawa, Yasutsune Itosu is better known as Anko Itosu. He had a very strict upbringing, and some stories say that when he was just a child, his father would beat him to make his body strong and his spirit aggressive. Although this was very cruel and is totally unacceptable to us now, it just may have worked for him. Itosu's physique is said to have become so rock hard that when he was struck, his opponents would simply bounce off him, their blows having had no effect whatsoever.

Along with his great friend Yasutsune Azato, he went to study Shuri-te directly under the renowned and legendary Master Sokon 'Bushi' Matsumura. With his unusual strength, Itosu soon became an extremely powerful karateka, famous for his destructive strikes, immensely strong grip, and huge chest.

One story claims that whilst conditioning his hands by striking a wall-mounted Makiwara (straw-covered striking post), he punched so hard that he actually knocked a hole through the wall! Others claim to have seen him crush green bamboo with his immense grip, which is an amazing feat when you consider that green bamboo is as hard as steel and used as scaffolding in the Orient!

Despite Itosu's strength and power, Matsumura did not approve of his young student. As far as he was concerned, relying on a strong body to withstand blows was foolish and no substitute for speed, skill, and the use of 'Tai Sabaki' (Body Movement). He famously said to him, "With your strong punch you can knock anything down, but you can't so much as touch me."

Not one to be easily deterred, Itosu left Matsumura's instruction and continued his training firstly with Master Nagahama and, when he died, with Master Gusukuma of Tomari. With Gusukuma's guidance, Itosu's strength and power developed and he became legendary in Okinawa, as did his style of Karate. There are many amazing stories of his fights including, like Matsumura, a match with a bull. It was Master Gusukuma who taught Itosu that everyone should adapt Karate to suit their own body type.

Too many instructors expect their students to have the same skills and abilities as themselves, which is impossible. A tall man will have different skills and abilities to a short man; a large man's skills and abilities will not be the same as a slighter man, and so on. Everyone has their own unique strengths and weaknesses. We should endeavour to make our strengths even stronger and work doubly hard to try and overcome our weaknesses. This attitude should be applied to all facets of our lives and not just Karate.

31
Itosu Takes the Bull by the Horns

It was a glorious Okinawan spring morning, and Anko Itosu was making his way home from an all-night Karate lesson with Master Matsumura. Having walked his best friend Yasutsune Azato home, he was now running a little late for work, so he decided to take a short cut he knew across a field. It was a short cut he had taken many times before and the field was hardly ever used by the farmer who owned it; that is until this particular day.

As he casually crossed the field, soaking up the morning sunshine and enjoying the coolness of the dew on his bare, training-sore feet, he became aware of a presence approaching him from a tree-shaded corner of the field behind and to the left of him. Without turning round, he increased his pace to a quick march and, sure enough, whoever was behind him did the same.

It sounded like there were a couple of them, and judging by the heavy sound of their footfalls, they were big guys too! Itosu, however, enjoyed a challenge and decided that if they wished to fight him then he would kindly oblige. Turning sharply on his heels to confront his stalkers, Itosu let out a mighty kiai, hoping that it would scare his assailants as it had done for Master Matsumura in the past. Itosu nearly choked on his kiai and his eyes just about popped out of his head at the immense and terrifying sight that confronted him.

A little more than ten feet from him stood the most massive bull the young Itosu had ever seen in his entire life. His sudden movement and short-lived kiai had temporarily halted the bull. Now, though, it lowered its enormous head so that its horns, each at least three feet long, almost touched the ground. It snorted a huge bellow of air from its lungs, blasting dust into the air, and began pawing the ground menacingly. With a powerful jackhammer of a stamp and a final huge snort that sent a shower of snot from its flaring nostrils, coating and flattening the grass beneath, the mighty animal prepared to charge.

Itosu, remaining as cool as possible under the circumstances, raised his hands and in a low, slightly shaky voice attempted to calm the animal as he slowly backed away. "Sshh. There's a g-good b-boy. N-nice bully. Stay there n-now. G-good boy." But for every step back Itosu took, the bull stomped, snorted, and advanced towards him. Itosu realized that his calming ploy was not going to work and that he was going to have to quickly think of something else.

At that moment, the hulk of a beast made his mind up for him as it let out the most terrifying and ear-splitting bellow, startling Itosu into action. The bull began a thundering charge, and as quick as a flash, Itosu spun round and shot like a bullet towards the perimeter wall, which was an agonizing thirty or so meters from him.

Beneath him the ground shook as the massive weight of the hulking, muscular beast sent shockwaves through the earth. Up ahead, Itosu noticed the heads of a group of boys appear above the wall. They had been engaged in a game of 'Tegumi' (Okinawan wrestling), which had been disturbed by the commotion coming from the field. Curiosity getting the better of them, they now stood on top of the wall, jumping up and down and waving their arms like a flock of frantic frogs, screaming for Itosu to run faster.

"Not far now. I'm nearly there. Come on, Anko, you can do it!" Itosu encouraged and willed himself toward the sanctuary of the wall. Closer and closer Itosu was getting to safety, but closer and closer the bull was getting to Itosu. He was sure he could feel the thundering beast's breath on his back and the tips of its horns tickling his bare feet.

The lads on the wall screamed louder, their eyes almost popping from their heads with the effort and excitement. "He's not going to make it!" one of them cried.

Seeing how close the bull now was to the fleeing man, they fell silent, each boy holding his breath, frozen like statues in terrified anticipation of what was about to happen to poor Itosu.

"Come on; only twenty feet to go. You're going to make it, Anko! You're going to—" Itosu's celebrations were cut rudely short when the bull's left horn clipped his foot and sent him careering through the air, causing his young spectators to gasp as one. Itosu instinctively went into a forward roll and immediately back onto his feet, as he had done a thousand times in training. He now had his back to the wall and was facing the giant animal bearing down on him.

With the reactions of a cat, he dived to his right. The bull's momentum was so great that it could not stop and continued headlong towards the wall.

"JUMP!" one of the lads screamed to his mates, rousing them from their petrified state. In the nick of time, they all managed to spring clear as the bull collided with the wall, sending stones the size of melons hurtling dangerously through the air. Displaying utter disregard for their safety, the boys then gingerly clambered back over the toppled stone so as not to miss the conclusion of this amazing chase.

The blurry-eyed bull, still slightly dazed from the incredible force of its impact with the wall, had now turned to face Itosu, who, puffing and panting, wiped the salty, stinging sweat from his eyes. He desperately needed to get over the wall to safety, but his bovine nemesis was now blocking the way. Itosu had to act now before the bull fully regained its senses.

What Itosu did next made his young audience gasp with both wonder and admiration. Mustering every ounce of courage he possessed, Itosu took a deep, calming breath and ran straight up to the bewildered beast and grabbed each of its horns. Then, with his famous strength, he began turning the dazed animal's head upward, hoping to topple it to the ground. The transfixed audience of children went wild, bursting into a frenzied chorus of encouraging shouts and cheers.

Itosu also started to scream and shout at the bull, "I am Itosu, the strongest man on all Okinawa! I am stronger than any man! I am stronger than any horse! I am stronger than any bull! Ahhhhh!"

The bull took up the challenge, and just as Itosu was beginning to look like he would turn the beast over, it began to fight back. With the benefit of quickly returning faculties and its enormous neck muscles, the bull forced its head back round until it was looking right into the eyes of Itosu as if to say, "You are not as strong as this bull, puny human!"

Itosu had to regain the upper hand somehow, and once again, to his admiring audience's amazement, he found a way. Holding onto its horns for dear life, he returned the bull's glare, and with a final, defiant cry of, "I am stronger than any bull!" he pushed back on the horns, let out a mighty kiai, and then, driving his entire body forward, he head-butted the animal right between the eyes.

Although he was now a little dazed himself, with an almighty effort, Itosu wrenched the animal's head round and it finally crashed to the ground, sending up a choking cloud of dust. As quick as a flash, Itosu used the bull's prone body like a springboard. Running up on to it, he bounced off its enormous ribcage, and leaped the wall in one bound. The dazed and exhausted Itosu was instantly mobbed by the group of admiring children, who rewarded him with cheers and rapturous applause.

On the other side of the wall, the baffled bull struggled to its feet and walked in a wobbly, rather drunken fashion back to the shaded corner of the field, where, I'm pleased to say, it made a full recovery.

I'm sure that if Master Matsumura had seen how quickly Itosu had run on that day, he would no longer think him too slow.

32
Pick on Someone Your Own Age

Anko Itosu, like Matsumura and Sakugawa before him, went on to serve the Royal Government of Okinawa. Through the influence of his friend Yasutsune Azato, he became the King's private secretary. He was highly respected amongst the people, not only for his prominent position and his incredible Karate prowess but also for his friendly, amiable personality. Unfortunately, there were then, as there are now, silly young men who thought that they were wiser and tougher than the older generation.

One such young man was a local hotheaded bully named Goro. Such was his arrogance that he thought he was already a greater fighter than many of the older, more experienced men in Shuri, and in a cruel manner had set out to prove it. The cowardly bully would wait until dark and pounce upon his elderly victims when they weren't looking to give them no chance whatsoever. He would then brag to his friends that he had beaten this Master or that Master in a fair fight.

Of all the Karate Masters on Okinawa, probably the most highly regarded was Anko Itosu. No matter whom Goro had mugged, for that was what he was doing, his friends would always tease him, saying, "Ah, but you haven't beaten old Itosu yet. He is the greatest fighter on the island, and until you defeat him you will only ever be second best."

Perhaps it was because Goro knew that Itosu was the better karateka that he had not yet tried to attack the old man. However, having had just about enough of all the teasing and goading that he could take, he decided it was time to sort out Itosu and save face with his cronies.

Being the conniving coward that he was, Goro thought up a plan that would give him the greatest chance of victory. Hearing that Itosu was going to a party with some friends and knowing that the sociable senior enjoyed a drink or two, Goro knew exactly what he would do.

Sneaking in the shadows so as not to be seen, Goro followed old Itosu to the party. Ensuring he had a view of the door, he then hid behind an out building, made himself comfortable, and like a spider having spun its web, he laid patiently in wait for his prey. Several hours and several cups of sake (rice wine) later, Itosu emerged from the party, stumbling through the door and singing at the top of his booming voice. He was obviously drunk and, better still for Goro, he was alone.

"This is going to be easier than I thought," Goro whispered to himself, grinning and rubbing his hands together. Silently, he set off behind the old man, cruelly stalking him along the unlit lane.

Once or twice, the old man stopped and took a quick, precautionary look behind to see if anyone was following him. Each time he did this it sent Goro's cold heart racing at the thought of being confronted face to face by the great Master. He didn't want to give Itosu any chance of defending himself at all.

Closer and closer Goro crept, his footsteps as light as a sparrow's, until he was within an arm's length of his poor victim. Any sound that he might have made to alert Itosu to his presence was completely drowned out by the merry old man's singing and occasional rasping belch.

Goro, satisfied that he was now close enough, drew back his right hand, and with his fist tightly clenched, launched his attack with a powerful punch into Itosu's back. The punch, which would have floored any other man, did not cause Itosu to miss even one step. His legendary physique was still as hard as nails, and to Goro's astonishment, Itosu did not even acknowledge his presence as he casually carried on walking and singing his way home.

Goro threw another punch, and again it appeared to go unnoticed by Itosu. The younger man's blood began to boil, as he was frustrated and embarrassed by his apparent weakness. Then he completely lost his temper and along with it all control. With a final mighty effort, he charged at Itosu, shouting and screaming at the top of his voice.

This time, rather than take the full force of Goro's punch, wily old Itosu casually stepped to one side, avoiding the punch and trapping Goro's right hand under his left arm. Without even looking at his attacker, Itosu then proceeded to pull the befuddled bully along the street whilst still singing at the top of his voice.

The confused and tiring youth feebly used his free hand to punch and claw at Itosu in a vain attempt to escape from the Master's vice-like grip. Again, Itosu completely ignored the blows and continued his journey home, carrying Goro under his arm as if he were an umbrella or a newspaper. Goro now looked a very sorry and ridiculous sight indeed as he hung limply from Itosu's grip with his feet trailing out behind him.

Now resigned to the ridicule he knew he would receive from his peers, he pleaded with Itosu. "Please, Master, please. I am sorry. Let me go and I will never do anything like this again, I promise. Please, Master Itosu!"

Dragging Goro for just a little while longer to ensure that the fool had learned his lesson, Itosu caught the young man's wrist in his powerful grip and asked, "Who are you anyway?"

"I am Goro, Master Itosu," he replied.

Itosu nodded and knowingly smiled at him, simply replying, "Ah, I see. Well, Goro, you really shouldn't play mean tricks on old men." Releasing the boy's wrist, he continued his walk home.

Watching Itosu disappear into the darkness still merrily singing, Goro, finally ashamed and embarrassed with his behaviour, had learned a valuable lesson and never bothered any men, old or young, ever again.

33
Old Itosu and the Judo Master

Itosu's well-proven reputation didn't allow him any respite from younger challengers, even at the ripe old age of seventy-five. There was always someone wanting to add the kudos of his name to their list of victories. One such person was a Japanese Judo player who was at least half Itosu's age and eager to prove Judo's superiority over Karate.

He challenged Itosu to a match, and I'd imagine that he was probably a little surprised when the old man accepted. News of the match spread quickly throughout Shuri and immediately caused a tremendous stir. The Japanese residents supported the Judo player, as Judo is a great Japanese martial art. The Okinawan people, of course, got behind their own hero, Anko Itosu. As the match approached, great excitement and a not too friendly rivalry developed between the two separate camps.

The day of the fight arrived and a massive crowd gathered in an ancient castle ruin, which served as the arena. Amongst the expectant audience the conversation all centred on whether the elderly Itosu should even attempt to fight the much younger and fitter Judo-ka.

"Old Itosu has bitten off more than he can chew this time," someone shouted.

"Yes, he must be crazy!" answered another.

"Everyone knows that Judo is far more effective than Karate," someone began stirring from the Japanese camp.

"Rubbish! Karate is by far the more superior fighting system." An Okinawan fan took the bait and an argument erupted amongst the fans.

"What do you know anyway?"

"Ah, shut up!"

"No, you shut up!"

Arguments began to break out throughout the crowd, spreading until a cacophony of deafening shouting and chanting from the two camps could be heard for miles around.

Unnoticed by the preoccupied crowd, the Judo player entered the arena, arms held arrogantly aloft like a victorious Roman gladiator, expecting adoration from his fans. Embarrassed by his apparent invisibility, he began to circle his arms as if limbering up his muscles in an attempt to hide his disappointment at the lack of attention he had just received. Then someone in the crowd shouted, "He's here! Yes! Look he's here!"

The Judo-ka smiled and once again threw his arms up, only to have his ego trodden on once again.

"Itosu is coming. It's Itosu!" The vast majority of the spectators burst into a spontaneous chant of "Itos-u, Itos-u, Itos-u," as the elderly Master strolled into the arena, smiling and politely bowing to the crowd on the way.

Approaching the younger man, Itosu bowed and politely introduced himself. "Good day, Master. I am Anko Itosu. Please allow me to extend my best wishes to you. I hope it will be an enjoyable and honourable match."

The Judo-ka, without even returning Itosu's rei (bow), looked at the crowd, laughed very rudely, and shouted for everyone to hear, "This is no match, you crazy old man! I will try to finish you quickly without hurting you too much."

Both the Okinawan and Japanese contingent in the crowd were disgusted at the younger man's flagrant show of disrespect, and nearly all of them began booing and jeering at him. Embarrassed at having turned his own people against him, the Judo-ka turned to Itosu and hissed, "Let's get on with this."

Again, Itosu bowed respectfully, and this time his opponent, hoping to regain favour with his audience, returned it. Itosu now took up a fighting stance and allowed the Judo-ka to approach him. The younger man had to find a way through Itosu's guard to grab his clothing, for Judo is useless unless this is achieved. The instant he was within range, and before the Judo-ka could grab him, Itosu unleashed a lightning-fast and incredibly powerful punch to his stomach. The force of the blow was so great that it knocked the wind clear out of his lungs, reducing him to a wheezing, gasping heap.

The crowd went wild, cheering for their elderly hero as he once again politely bowed to his opponent and proceeded to deliver first aid to him until he was able to stand. Ensuring that the younger man was in good health, Itosu then simply turned and left the arena as he had entered, smiling and politely bowing to the crowd on his way.

34

The Importance of Itosu

Anko Itosu, perhaps more than any other person past or present, has had a profound influence on the development and spread of Karate in a number of ways.

He is credited with the creation of the Pinan or Heian group of kata, which forms the basis of much of Karate now taught. Naihanchi 2 and 3, also known as Tekki Nidan and Tekki Sandan, are also credited to him.

In 1902, along with his student Gichin Funakoshi, he organized the first public demonstration of China Hand, as it was then known, for some prominent Navy dignitaries and their crew. It was after this demonstration that word began to spread to Japan about this mysterious Okinawan fighting art, and other demonstrations were to follow, including one for the visiting Crown Prince.

Itosu was a firm believer that Karate should benefit the physical and mental development of all the Japanese Empire and not just Okinawa. So in October 1908, he sent a letter to the Ministry of Education and the Ministry of War which contained his now famous 'Ten Precepts of

China Hand'. As a result of his letter and the public demonstrations that he organized, Karate was, in a simplified form, soon to be added to the school and university physical education curriculum of both Okinawa and Japan.

Some of Itosu's students went on to become some of the greatest and most influential men in the history of Karate, creating several of the most popular styles practised today. Itosu's final contribution before he died in 1915 at the age of eighty-five was to encourage his students, such as Gichin Funakoshi, to travel to Japan to pass on their knowledge of Karate.

35
Itosu's Ten Precepts of China Hand

There have been many translations of Itosu's 1908 letter. The version below was commissioned by and is used with the very kind permission of Sensei Iain Abernethy.* Do not dwell too much on trying to understand the language used in the precepts. For now it is enough that you understand what an important piece of Karate history this letter truly is.

Karate did not develop from Buddhism or Confucianism. In the past the Shorin-ryu school and the Shorei-ryu school were brought to Okinawa from China. Both of these schools have strong points and I therefore list them below just as they are without embellishment.

1. *Karate is not merely practised for your own benefit; it can be used to protect one's family or master. It is not intended to be used against a single assailant but instead as a way of avoiding injury by using the hands and feet should one by any chance be confronted by a villain or ruffian.*

---

* Please visit www.iainabernethy.com Sensei Abernethy's website provides a detailed explanation of Itosu's precepts.

2. *The purpose of Karate is to make the muscles and bones hard as rock and to use the hands and legs as spears. If children were to begin training naturally in military prowess while in elementary school, then they would be well suited for military service. Remember the words attributed to the Duke of Wellington after he defeated Napoleon, "Today's battle was won on the playing fields of our schools".*

3. *Karate cannot be quickly learned. Like a slow-moving bull, it eventually travels a thousand leagues. If one trains diligently for one or two hours every day, then in three or four years one will see a change in physique. Those who train in this fashion will discover the deeper principles of Karate.*

4. *In Karate, training of the hands and feet are important, so you should train thoroughly with a makiwara. In order to do this, drop your shoulders, open your lungs, muster your strength, grip the floor with your feet, and concentrate your energy into your lower abdomen. Practise using each arm one to two hundred times each day.*

5. *When you practise the stances of Karate, be sure to keep your back straight, lower your shoulders, put strength in your legs, stand firmly, and drop your energy into your lower abdomen.*

6. *Practise each of the techniques of Karate repeatedly. Learn the explanations of every technique well, and decide when and in what manner to apply them when needed. Enter, counter, withdraw is the rule for torite [releasing hand].*

7. *You must decide if Karate is for your health or to aid your duty.*

8. *When you train, do so as if on the battlefield. Your eyes should glare, shoulders drop, and body harden. You should always train with intensity and spirit as if actually facing the enemy, and in this way you will naturally be ready.*

9. *If you use up your strength to excess in Karate training, this will cause you to lose the energy in your lower abdomen and will be harmful to your body. Your face and eyes will turn red. Be careful to control your training.*

10. *In the past, many masters of Karate have enjoyed long lives. Karate aids in developing the bones and muscles. It helps the digestion as well as the circulation. If Karate should be introduced, beginning in the elementary schools, then we will produce many men each capable of defeating ten assailants.*

If the students at teacher training college learn Karate in accordance with the above precepts and then, after graduation, disseminate this to elementary schools in all regions, within 10 years Karate will spread all over Okinawa and to mainland Japan. Karate will therefore make a great contribution to our military. I hope you will seriously consider what I have written here—Anko Itosu, October 1908.

36
Yasutsune Azato—the Mysterious Master

"Certainly he was without equal in all Okinawa." This is how Gichin Funakoshi described his inspirational instructor Master Yasutsune Azato. High praise indeed when you consider that Funakoshi also spent twenty or so years under the instruction of Azato's closest friend, the legendary Itosu.

Born in 1828, Azato was a man of high standing, being Lord of the village of Asato and King Sho Tai's closest military adviser. A student of Bushi Matsumura, he excelled at Karate, was an accomplished swordsman, and a brilliant horseman.

Despite his position and accomplishments, when he died in Tokyo in 1902 he left very little of himself to posterity. There are no known pictures or portraits of him and the only written accounts of his life are those written by his student Gichin Funakoshi.

A possible reason for this could be his support of the Meiji Government and its plans for the Japanese Empire. This is a complicated subject, but simply put, during the Meiji Restoration, the Emperor and his government set about modernising Japan. To do this, they outlawed some old-fashioned traditions in favour of more modern, Western ideas.

One of the oldest and strongest traditions in Okinawa and Japan was the wearing of the keimochi topknot. The men would grow long hair and tie it in a topknot, which was regarded as a sign of both position and masculinity. Azato had embraced the ideas of the Meiji Government wholeheartedly, and when the topknot was banned, he was the first man on Okinawa to shave his off. This may have enraged many of his more traditionally minded counterparts, who became known as the 'Obstinates' due to their refusal to succumb to government legislation.

It is possible, though not proven, that some of these people may not have wanted Azato to be remembered or recognized for being the great politician and martial artist that he was. So when Azato eventually moved permanently to Japan, all that seemed to remain of him were the memories of his closest friends like Itosu and Funakoshi.

If not for Funakoshi's written tributes to the man, of whom he said, *"Without a doubt the greatest part of my knowledge of Karate is based on the instruction I received from him"*, the name of Yasutsune Azato may have been erased from history permanently.

37
With Hands Mightier Than a Sword

Although they were great friends, Azato, like Matsumura, did not agree with Itosu's policy of developing a hard body to withstand blows, as he felt that this would be extremely foolhardy against an armed opponent. Azato, being of a taller and slimmer build than his good friend, preferred the application of speed and tai sabaki or body movement to avoid attacks and overwhelm opponents. His expertise in tai sabaki helped him overcome perhaps his most formidable opponent.

Although he was a very modest man, he was also extremely confident in his ability, and rightly so. Gichin Funakoshi wrote that on one occasion Azato said to him, *"I doubt very much that I would lose to anyone in a fight to the death."* A hefty claim indeed!

Word of this private comment soon spread throughout the tiny island and was carried from village to village by gossiping traders and travellers, then expanded on and drunkenly exaggerated in the island's many taverns. Like a Chinese whisper, every time the comment was repeated, a little bit got added or altered.

"Azato says he could beat anyone in a fight to the death."

"Azato says he's never lost in a fight to the death." OBVIOUSLY!

"Azato says he's beaten a hundred men in fights to the death."

"Azato says he could beat a swordsman even if he were unarmed!"

"Azato once beat three swordsmen whilst blindfolded and one arm tied behind his back."

And so on it went until word of Azato's amazing and vastly exaggerated feats reached the ears of one of the greatest swordsmen on Okinawa, Yorin Kanna.

Kanna was a mountain of a man with massive shoulders and said to be two stories high; his neck was so wide and muscular that it appeared as if his head were placed directly onto his shoulders; his biceps were as big as grapefruit, and his forearms were as large as an average man's thighs; his legs were as wide as the mightiest oak tree, displaying muscles upon muscles upon even more muscles. Fearless, brave, hugely aggressive with a true warrior spirit, his awesome appearance usually defeated his opponents before actual combat had even commenced.

When the vastly exaggerated word of Azato's outrageous comments finally reached Kanna, he was furious. "Who does this Azato think he is making such ridiculous claims?" he blasted. "He has gone too far. I, Yorin Kanna, am the mightiest swordsman on all Okinawa, and I will challenge him to a match. Then we will see just how good he is."

Although Azato could have explained to Kanna that he hadn't actually made the comments that had been bandied around, he did not. Instead, he immediately accepted Kanna's challenge with great pleasure. Azato knew that despite Kanna's well-grounded claims to be the greatest swordsman on Okinawa, he too was a superior and extraordinary exponent of the long blade. However, to prove his superiority, Azato had something a little special in mind for Kanna.

The match was a private affair held at dawn in a secret location with only Master Azato, Master Kanna, and a small number of their closest friends in attendance. The two men stood with their respective companions at opposite sides of the designated fighting area. Kanna was the first of the two men to make his way into the centre of the area and prepare for battle. Azato, on the other hand, appeared to be having quite an intense and heated conversation with one of his companions, who appeared to be in some distress over something.

Kanna smiled to himself and thought, 'They are afraid of me as is everyone. I have already won.' In a confident and somewhat sarcastic tone of voice, he called to Azato, "Hey, mighty Azato, come on. Are you here to fight me or to squabble with your men?"

Azato glanced toward the huge form of Kanna and answered, "One moment, if you please, Kanna." He then took his companion by the shoulders and whispered something in his ear. His companion, obviously still very perturbed about something, stepped away, bowed to Azato, and turning to face the hulking figure of Kanna, shouted, "My master is ready."

"About time!" exclaimed Kanna, and he drew his sword. Azato walked boldly towards Kanna, stopped a few feet from him and bowed respectfully. Kanna returned the bow, then for the first time noticed that Azato was not armed. "Where is your sword?" he asked.

"My hands and my feet are my swords, Master Kanna," Azato replied coolly.

Kanna nonchalantly shrugged his shoulders and coldly replied, "Very well; it's your funeral."

"Indeed," was the smiling Azato's only response as he dropped into a 'kokutsa dachi' (back stance) and extended his arms out in front of himself. Behind Azato, Kanna noticed his opponent's concerned companion wince and turn away, unable to watch his friend's unbelievable lunacy.

The sun was behind Kanna, its reflection off his swaying blade almost completely blinding Azato. Bouncing lightly on his toes, like a swallow in flight, Azato began to dart left and right, forward and back, distracting his opponent whilst circling him to reverse their position to the sun.

Suddenly realizing his nimble-footed nemesis's intention, Kanna let out a fierce kiai and raised his sword above his head. Stepping towards Azato, he fiercely sliced the blade diagonally downwards at incredible speed, fully expecting to cut Azato in two. This was not to be, for as Kanna raised his sword, Azato moved in quickly, deflecting the swordsman's strike. Then, using his attacker's momentum, Azato took Kanna's arms and threw the muscle-bound man-mountain. Utterly disoriented, Kanna found himself performing an involuntary forward summersault, landing heavily onto the flat on his back.

Azato turned to his initially reluctant companion and gave him a cheeky wink and a smile as if to say, "See, I told you. Now chill out!"

His mouth hanging open in total disbelief at what he had just witnessed, all his friend could manage was a strained nod and quick double thumbs-up. 'Perhaps all the incredible rumours were true after all!' he thought.

Winded, confused, embarrassed, and infuriated, Kanna struggled to his feet and took hold of the sword he had dropped during his flight. His blood was boiling, surging through his body so much that the veins in his massive neck resembled an erupted volcano's lava flow. Again he raised his sword, let out a blood-curdling battle cry, and with full commitment and the deadly intention to slay his cocky counterpart, he attacked.

The result was exactly the same, as Azato, calmly and with no apparent effort, moved in, parried the strike, and threw Kanna to the ground. Time and time again, Kanna launched himself at Azato, only to find he was gazing up at the sky on his dew-soaked back. Mentally and physically exhausted from over an hour of relentless but ultimately fruitless attacking, the mighty Yorin Kanna could do nothing else but concede defeat to the better man.

Azato's doubtful friend ran to him completely overwhelmed, overjoyed, and overexcited at his master's impossible victory. "How did you do it, Master? I never believed it would be possible! How did you do it?"

Azato explained. "Kanna is a brave and powerful warrior used to overwhelming his opponents. He attacks with full zeal and intent with no regard or thought for his safety and completely unaware if he is being baited. For this reason his attacks were easy to read and predict."

Perhaps another reason for the ease of his victory was Azato's knowledge of Kanna before the fight took place. It is said that Azato kept details of all the great martial artists on Okinawa, and not just their names and addresses. He had information about their favourite weapons, styles, weaknesses, strengths, and their character. As the mighty samurai warrior Sun Tzu once wrote: *"If you know your enemy and know yourself, you need not fear the result of a hundred battles."*

38
The Importance of Azato

Master Azato, like all the previous masters discussed, had an extraordinarily long life for people of this time, dying in 1906 aged seventy-eight. Azato was a great martial artist in his own right, maybe the greatest of all, if we believe his student Gichin Funakoshi.

Gichin Funakoshi credits Azato for the vast majority of his Karate knowledge, and it is mainly because of Funakoshi that we know anything of Azato at all. Funakoshi himself is widely recognized as the man who initiated the worldwide popularization of Karate, so we could say that he is Azato's greatest legacy, and it is he we shall find out about next.

39

Gichin Funakoshi—An Eventful Year

1868 was an extremely eventful and important year indeed for both the Japanese Empire and the future of Karate-Do. In Tokyo, the capital of Japan, the Meiji Government came to power and began its quest for a new, more modern country, embracing Western culture and ideas from Europe and the United States of America. At that very same time in Shuri, the royal capital of Okinawa, a baby boy was born who was destined to grow up and be the man responsible for the incredible worldwide growth of a new sporting phenomenon called Karate. That boy's name was Gichin Funakoshi.

It became evident from a very young age that Funakoshi was a particularly frail, sickly child, and sadly, those close to him did not expect Gichin to have a very long life. Thankfully, fate had other ideas for the young Funakoshi, when at school at eleven years old, he befriended the son of the great Karate Master Yasutsune Azato.

Funakoshi and young Azato would spend hours at each other's homes studying their schoolwork and playing their favourite game, Tegumi, with other friends under the watchful eye of Azato and his close friend Anko Itosu. Despite his frail health and small stature, little Funakoshi had tremendous spirit and guile, and somehow always seemed to be able to outmanoeuvre his bigger, stronger playmates.

Master Azato grew very fond of his son's new friend and decided to teach Funakoshi a few Karate exercises on his visits to help strengthen his muscles and hopefully improve his delicate health. Young Funakoshi showed true dedication and determination, and quite miraculously, after just a few months of practising a little Karate, he was visibly transforming into a fitter, healthier, and for his small size, a very strong boy.

40
Azato's Amazing Offer

Hugely impressed by the incredible progress and fighting spirit of his son's best friend, the great Master Azato decided that he would do something that he had never even considered before. One evening whilst watching the boys at their usual rough-and-tumble game of Tegumi, he ordered them to stop and come and sit with him for a while.

"Boys," Master Azato announced, "I have decided it is time for me to pass on my knowledge of the Tode to someone I feel is worthy."

The two boys looked at each other silently, both thinking that this meant he would be teaching his one and only son the fighting tradition of the Azato family.

The boys were left drop-jawed in astonishment as Master Azato continued. "Gichin, I would like that person to be you. What do you think? Do you accept my offer?" Gichin did not know what to say and he felt more than just a little uncomfortable that Master Azato had not asked his son, who sat beside him looking quite dejected and upset. "Well, boy, speak up. What do you say?"

"Master Azato, I am greatly honoured at your generous offer but—"

"But! But what, Gichin?" Azato interrupted, sounding most irritated.

His voice trembling with nerves, Funakoshi continued. "But surely your son would be a far better choice, Master Azato. He is far stronger, better skilled and—"

"Nonsense!" Azato exclaimed. "Everyone knows how difficult it is for a parent to teach his own child anything! Although I love him dearly, there would be arguing and sulking. I would lose my temper with him, and then his mother would lose her temper with me. It would be impossible! I will teach you and then you will have the responsibility of teaching my son. How does that sound?"

Funakoshi turned to face young Azato, looking and hoping for his approval, for he would not sacrifice their friendship for Master Azato. "What do you say, my friend? It will be fun, and I will see even more of you now, and together we can become great fighters like your father."

Young Azato, who had been staring at the floor to hide his tears, slowly raised his head and, wiping the moisture from his eyes with his sleeve, looked up towards Funakoshi. For several unbearable seconds he stared stone-faced into Funakoshi's eyes, then realizing what a special friendship they had, he gave a nod of his head accompanied by a broad smile of agreement. Funakoshi then sprang to his feet and giving Master Azato a deep rei, he accepted his generous and unexpected offer. Gichin Funakoshi was to be Master Azato's only ever student.

41
Nosey Neighbours

Teaching and learning Karate on Okinawa at this time was no simple matter. There were no large Karate schools on every street corner, as there are today, and Karate was still an illegal art on the island at this time. For Funakoshi to study with Master Azato, he had to wait until darkness fell and walk several miles through unlit and quite dangerous streets. After the long walk, he would then train for several hours before walking all the way back in the early hours of the morning and go to school for the day. All this at the tender age of just eleven years!

Quite soon, the people of his neighbourhood began to notice the strange nighttime comings and goings of the Funakoshi boy. Curiosity got the better of some them and they would ask prying questions of him. "Out for a walk again tonight, Gichin?"

"Yes," he would simply answer, moving along as quickly as possible and trying his best to ignore any further prying.

"Would you like some company, Gichin?"

"Oh, no thank you. I am going for a very, very long walk and I'm sure you wouldn't enjoy it," he would deflect.

"But it is pouring with rain, Gichin. Why would anyone want to walk in this rain?"

"I enjoy walking in the rain. It is refreshing and saves having to bathe!" he would reply, attempting to evade his nosey neighbours' interrogations and quickly scuttling away before anyone could follow him.

It's not that he wanted to lie to his friends and neighbours, but due to the illegal nature of his lessons, he did not want to get himself or Master Azato into any trouble. However, neighbours and close-knit communities being what they are, the locals soon created rumours, gossip, and conjecture, deciding for themselves what Funakoshi's peculiar nocturnal activities actually were. Considering his young age, the most common rumour was completely ridiculous! Huddling together so as not to be heard, they would watch Gichin set off on his nightly excursions and whisper to each other.

"I've heard that he is spending his evenings with … Sshh, come closer," they would say if the boy looked their way. "I've heard he is spending his nights … ahem … drinking, gambling, and in the company of women!"

"No! Never! I don't believe it! He is so young! Why don't his parents do something about it! Disgusting! Disgraceful! Despicable!"

Although the rumours were completely untrue, they did have the benefit of giving young Funakoshi the highest street cred and kudos amongst the other boys in the town, which he rather enjoyed.

42

Do It Again, Funakoshi!

Master Azato was a very hard taskmaster, only allowing young Funakoshi a few minutes' rest and a quick drink of water after his long walk before beginning his lesson. Training was held in the back yard enclosed by a high fence and under a dim lamp light no matter how good or bad the weather. Master Azato would sit on the veranda, often joined by his great friend and Karate genius Master Itosu, and together they would watch Funakoshi perform Tekki kata.

On completion of the kata, Masters Azato and Itosu never gave the boy any praise for a job well done, but one or other of them would just bark the order, "Do it again, Funakoshi!" time after time. In fact, Funakoshi would often be made to repeat Tekki over one hundred times in a single lesson, until Azato was satisfied that his exhausted young protégé understood it thoroughly. The only sign that the great man gave that he was satisfied with Funakoshi's performance of the kata was a sharp downward nod of his head, which also signified that the lesson was over. Azato would then send the boy off on his long, tedious trudge back home.

Nowadays, karateka have to learn many different kata to progress through the various grades. Compare this to Funakoshi, who for the first three years of his training did Tekki kata and nothing but Tekki kata. After three years, Master Azato allowed Funakoshi to learn additional techniques, but he was not taught a new kata for a further six years!

I doubt very much that many Karate students today possess the patience and steely determination required to constantly repeat a single kata over such an incredibly long period in a world where quick results are now the order of the day. Remember that every kata is a record of a complete fighting system, and the early Karate Masters may have only mastered two or three kata in their whole lifetime. For this reason, they intimately understood the meaning of every tiny movement of every technique and how to use them in real life-and-death situations.

For a karateka today to attain the coveted black belt and beyond, they have to learn up to twenty-six kata, which is no small achievement in itself, as it requires memorizing many hundreds of techniques. It is an unfortunate result of having to learn so many kata, though, that very few modern-day karateka ever truly learn the real meaning behind the techniques as the old Masters did. If you are a karateka, try studying your favourite kata thoroughly for a while and see how many uses of each technique you can find, for there is far more to each move than first appears.

43
Fighting a Typhoon

There are no fantastic tales of Funakoshi ever defeating marauding pirates, felling raging bulls, or testing his skills against other great martial artists. He was a kindly, mild-mannered, and peaceful man, whose biggest battles were always personal ones. He constantly strove for greater knowledge of Karate and to improve his physical and mental strength.

As already mentioned, Funakoshi spent the first nine years of his training practising just a single kata called Tekki. The word 'Tekki' means 'Iron Horse' and refers to 'kiba dachi' or 'horse riding stance', the only stance used in the entire kata. Imagine the shape your legs would make if you sat upon a large horse. Then take away the horse and maintain the same leg position whilst standing on the ground. Put a Stetson on and you would now resemble Yosemite Sam or the way cowboys walk in some westerns after a long ride on the cattle trail! That is how the kiba dachi stance from Tekki kata appears.

Although the stance seems relatively simple to perform, it requires a great deal of leg strength to maintain over an extended period, such as when performing kata. Funakoshi, being the keen, disciplined student that he was, always looked for new and inventive ways to practise and improve his stance. Whilst in kiba dachi, he would hold buckets of water, logs, or even his best friend young Azato aloft on his shoulders until his thighs felt as if they were on fire. These in themselves were arduous and tiring training methods, but they pale into insignificance compared to the ultimate means of testing kiba dachi that Funakoshi employed when the opportunity arose.

As previously mentioned, Okinawa is often described as the Island of Typhoons due to it being subjected regularly to these violent tropical storms. A typhoon's torrential rain can cause terrible floods and mudslides, and its hurricane-force winds rip trees from the earth and tear roofs from houses as if they were made of paper. The Okinawan people, having learned their lesson over many centuries, ensured that their homes were never more than a single storey high, that the roof tiles were cemented in place, and that the foundations were deep and strong.

One year, when Funakoshi had just about completed his first nine years' training, the typhoon season arrived with a vengeance. Rolling black clouds had been gathering all day and transformed day into night-like darkness. The wind had now reached its full howling and destructive crescendo, rattling shuttered windows and secured doors. Anything that wasn't tied down, and even some things that were, were sent hurtling along the deserted streets of Shuri. The plummeting rain, the wind not allowing it a direct route to earth, was driving horizontally into buildings and finding its way into the most watertight homes.

The Funakoshi household, along with the rest of Okinawa's population, had battened down the hatches and were huddling together in the safest corner of their home, waiting for the storm to subside. Gisu Funakoshi noticed that his son Gichin looked upset and concluded that he must be afraid of the terrible storm raging outside.

"Do not look so worried, my son. You've lived through dozens of typhoons, and you will survive this one. Why don't you come and sit with your mother and me?" he suggested, beckoning to the troubled-looking teenager.

"I am not worried about the storm hurting us, Father," Gichin replied curtly. "I am angry with it for disturbing my training. I should be with Masters Azato and Itosu now!"

"Does your Karate mean that much to you? Surely it won't hurt you to miss one day! Besides, why waste energy being angry with a storm? You can't fight Mother Nature, can you?" Gisu Funakoshi smiled lovingly at his son, thinking that he had calmed him, only for Gichin to spring to his feet with a wide-eyed defiant look upon his face.

"Actually, Father, yes I can!" he replied.

With his parents looking on in utter disbelief, he began to strip off all his clothes until he just stood in his underwear, displaying his muscular and wiry physique.

"What on earth are you doing?" cried his mother.

Lifting a tatami (straw) mat from the floor, Gichin turned to his parents and defiantly announced, "I am going to fight the typhoon." Before his dumbstruck parents could object, he marched through the door and out into the storm.

Outside, the typhoon was ravaging the town, and as soon as Gichin set foot on the veranda, the tatami mat he held caught the wind like a ship's sail. Lifting him at least eight feet in the air, the wind propelled him off the veranda and he somersaulted into the street, which had been transformed into a thick river of mud by the deluge. Still clinging to the mat, the tenacious teenager fought his way back to his feet, battling against the suction of the muddy embrace that held him.

With his back to the powerful wind and stinging rain, Funakoshi held the tatami mat by two end corners, and staying as low to the ground as he could, he began to drag it backwards to his house. After what seemed like an age, he managed to get around the side of the house where there was just a little shelter from the wind provided by a stone wall, which had so far been able to withstand the force of the storm.

Now standing on the tatami mat to prevent it from blowing away, Funakoshi began looking around the backyard for something to help him climb onto the roof. Shielding his eyes from the stinging watery bombardment with his forearm, he spotted what he was looking for, but the ladder was just out of arm's reach. Determined not to sacrifice the mat to the wind, he lay on top of it and, like a snake, slid on his belly until he could just reach the bottom rung of the ladder without losing contact with mat.

It took an almighty effort, but eventually a breathless Gichin managed to take hold of the ladder and pull it to the floor beside him. With the wind to his back, Gichin could at last use it to his advantage. Standing on the mat, he lifted the ladder and rested it against the low roof of the house. Carefully, he pulled the mat from beneath his feet in front of him, and using the wind like a kind of glue, pinned it up against the ladder.

Lifting and holding the tatami mat in front of him as he went, Funakoshi, rung by energy sapping rung, began to climb. Several times he almost fell from the ladder as he stretched out to save the mat from being blowing away. After what seemed like hours and against all the odds, the determined young man somehow managed to get both him and the tatami mat onto the roof.

For a minute or maybe two, Gichin just lay there on the roof of his house, clinging to the mat as he gulped in great lungfuls of air to recover from his exhausting struggle. Then, with a final deep breath, he slowly began to bring his knees up towards his chest. Ever so carefully, he managed to get to his feet, but remained in a low, crouched position. Then, spreading his feet outwards, he quite amazingly stood on top of the tatami mat in kiba dachi. The wind and rain conspired to drive Funakoshi off the roof and back into the muddy street.

Smiling and growing in confidence, Gichin carefully started to creep his bare feet off the tatami mat and he reached down to grab it by its edges. Fighting to maintain his footing, he began to lift the mat from the roof. Impossibly, he managed to get the tatami mat up to chest height before Mother Nature's elemental allies, the howling typhoon wind and blinding rain, caused Gichin to slip and hoisted both him and his mat up into the air. For nearly twenty metres, he spun and tumbled like an autumn leaf before he was unceremoniously dumped back into the muddy quagmire, which only hours before had been a busy and bustling street.

His lungs had already been bursting with the massive effort, but the heavy impact with terra firma had knocked the breath clean out of him, and both his nose and mouth were filled with mud. Pushing himself up onto his knees, Funakoshi wretched, coughed, spat, and snorted the invading mud from his nose and mouth as he desperately struggled to breathe.

Finally, and with great relief, he managed to draw in a long, wonderful, glorious, and life-saving breath. Now, for most people, that terrifying experience would have signalled to them that it was time to give up and get inside where it was safe and warm. Funakoshi, though, was not most people. Actually, covered in mud and leafy debris from the surrounding trees as he was, Funakoshi didn't look like a human at all, but rather like some strange alien being from a distant galaxy.

Displaying a stubborn defiance, Funakoshi turned to face his house and the typhoon. Raising his head and hands towards the sky, he released a blood-curdling kiai to inform the elements that he wasn't done yet. He then located and retrieved the tatami mat from the mud and resumed his crazy quest.

Inside, his parents, worried to distraction about their son, looked up towards the ceiling as they heard a loud thud above them.

"There it is again!" said a panic-stricken Mrs Funakoshi.

"Don't worry, darling. It's probably just a branch that has been torn from a tree," Gisu Funakoshi speculated.

"No, listen," replied his wife. "Something is moving around up there. A seagull perhaps?" At that moment there was another heavy thud from above.

"If that's a seagull, it's a really big one," replied Gisu, half jokingly.

"Then what on earth could be thumping around on the roof in this storm?" As the question escaped Mrs Funakoshi's lips, both she and her husband had the same terrifying realization.

"Gichin!" they screamed in unison, and scrambled towards the front door, tripping over each other in their bid to rescue their boy.

Emerging into the chaos of the storm, Funakoshi's parents were met by a dozen or more of their neighbours from across the street, who had witnessed nearly all of their son's amazing antics. As they trudged into the middle of the street, one of his neighbours took Gisu by the shoulders and pointed towards the roof of his house.

"Look!" he shouted, struggling to be heard above the howling of the wind. "Look, it is Gichin. On the roof! Look!"

The Funakoshis followed their neighbour's pointing finger and were stunned by what they saw. Their son, Gichin, his wild eyes wide and incredibly white, and his teeth looking even brighter against the darkness of his mud-covered body, was standing on their roof. Above his head he held on to the tatami mat, and like a man possessed was shouting and screaming victoriously at the top of his voice.

"That boy of yours is crazy!" the neighbour exclaimed.

A proud smile spread across Mr Funakoshi's face and he replied, "No, my son is not crazy. He has fought the typhoon and won. He can do anything now." Smiling, he turned to his wife and shouted, "See, I told you it wasn't a seagull."

A beaming Gisu Funakoshi then took a few steps towards his house and bowed deeply to his son before applauding him enthusiastically. He was quickly followed by his wife, and then one by one, all of their neighbours spontaneously joined in, cheering and whooping for Gichin Funakoshi, the boy who dared to fight a typhoon and won.

44
Time for Change

Gichin Funakoshi had always dreamed of entering medical school when he was a boy. Unfortunately for him, though, it was a requirement of the Meiji Government that all boys should shave off their topknot to enter university. Knowing how terribly upsetting this would be for his parents, who were strongly against many of the government's new laws, Funakoshi sacrificed his ambitions of being a doctor to maintain family harmony.

However, Funakoshi was hungry for knowledge and eventually succumbed to his ambitious nature. Risking the wrath of his parents, he finally removed his topknot and entered university to train to be a teacher. Itosu and Azato may have had some part to play in this decision, as they were avid supporters of Meiji and a huge influence over him.

His parents reacted exactly as he expected they would. His mother was so upset that she refused to even talk to Gichin for a week, whilst his father found it difficult to contain his anger whenever he looked at his boy's freshly cropped hair. However, as time passed and fewer and fewer boys wore the topknot, Funakoshi's parents' disappointment was replaced with pride in their son's tenacity and drive.

Gichin Funakoshi was now receiving most of his Karate instruction from Master Itosu. As we know, Itosu had proven his skill time and time again in many real fights by using Karate as the brutal and deadly form of self-defence it was designed to be. However, being the visionary man that he was, he now realized that for Karate to survive and be accepted in this new modern era, it would have to evolve and change into something less violent. It would now have to develop into an activity that would appeal to all age groups and, even more crucially, the government.

With the guidance of Itosu, Funakoshi began teaching Karate publicly for the first time as a means of physical exercise. They introduced students to the peaceful nature and mental philosophies of their beloved art. Making subtle changes to the kata and kumite techniques, Funakoshi and Itosu showed that Karate was a fantastic way to increase physical fitness, build a strong physique and a disciplined mind. It was still an effective means of self-defence, but Itosu and Funakoshi taught that violence should only ever be used as a last resort after all other means of avoiding a fight have been exhausted.

This philosophy of avoiding conflict is best explained in the following tale, which was told by Funakoshi in his book *Karate Do: My Way of Life*.

45
No Need for Violence

One particularly beautiful summer's evening, Itosu, Funakoshi, and several other students decided to take a stroll after a long, tough training session. There wasn't a cloud in the sky, so the full moon took centre stage, with a celestial dome of countless stars stretching uninterrupted to the horizon.

Master Itosu decided that they should go to a local teahouse, which had an outdoor garden with amazing cliff-top views of the ocean. It was well worth the mile-long walk and the group of men stood silently, tea in hand, open-mouthed, and awestruck at the picture-book scene that greeted them on their arrival.

The moon, appearing as if it had just risen from the sea, hung so low in the sky that you could almost imagine the last remnants of saltwater dripping off it. It cast golden moonbeams across the shimmering waters that stretched out like the huge tentacles of a mythical sea monster. The moonlight tentacles reached all the way to the coastline, as if the moon monster were trying to grab the island and drag it away for a great feast.

Every pockmarked lunar crater and mountain could be seen as clearly as if they had a moon map spread across a table in front of them. As if to add the finishing touch to a great artistic masterpiece, a flock of geese, flying in perfect V-formation, flew in front of the rising moon. With comic synchronicity, every one in the group let out a great sigh of satisfaction, and then, looking at each other, they burst into joyous laughter.

The men spent several more hours gazing at the moon and night sky, listening intently to Master Itosu's stories of the old Karate Masters and taking turns to recite poetry. Engrossed in their discussions and performances, the group completely lost any sense of time until the first cloud of the night passed across the moon. The sudden loss of celestial illumination had the same effect as an alarm clock, interrupting their chain of thought and snapping the moonstruck men out of the moment.

Master Itosu hoisted his large frame to its feet, smiled, and announced, "Come on, lads; this magical night has cast its spell and stolen time from us. We'd better make our way back."

With lanterns to light the dark road home, they reluctantly began their journey. The road was known to be treacherous after dark, as it had no lighting and cut through a thick pine forest, which provided ample cover for anyone with villainy in mind. This did not worry Itosu or any of his students, as they were all very useful karateka. With their spirits soaring and their mood relaxed from a wonderful evening spent together, the young men and their great teacher proceeded without a care in the world.

That is until one of the students suddenly hissed from the front of the group, "Sshh, be quiet!" Then added in a forced whisper, "Quickly put your lanterns out and stay silent."

"What is it, boy?" Itosu asked, making no attempt to keep quiet, as nothing frightened the great man.

"I think it may be a gang of bandits, Master!" the young man replied, his voice now quivering slightly with nerves and a rush of excitement, a sensation that each of the young men now shared.

They held their breath to be able to hear better and, sure enough, about one hundred metres ahead of them, a rowdy group of burly men burst from the cover of the trees.

"Should we confront them, Master?" asked Funakoshi.

"No, just stand with your backs to the moon, boys, and say nothing for now."

Funakoshi did not understand. 'Stand with our backs to the moon? What does he mean by that?' he thought.

Up ahead, the strangers could be seen talking and conspiring amongst themselves before turning to face Itosu and his young students. A large, brutish-looking fellow then stepped forward, and using his hand as a visor to shield his eyes from the moonlight, shouted at them with booze-slurred speech, "Hey, you, what are you doing on our road? Don't you know there's a toll to pay?" The brute's cronies sneered and sniggered behind their loutish leader.

"Master Itosu, this is preposterous!" exclaimed Funakoshi. "This is a public road. We should teach these ruffians a lesson!"

Funakoshi's comrades enthusiastically agreed with him, eager to put their martial skills to practical use. Some of them even began to limber up ready for action. However, Master Itosu had other ideas.

"Funakoshi, come here," he ordered.

Thinking that he was about to be sent into battle, Itosu's best student ran to his master, bowed and declared, "I am ready, Master Itosu."

"That's good, lad. Now go and talk to them and see if you can find out what their problem is."

Funakoshi was absolutely flabbergasted. "Talk to them, Master? Talk to them! Surely the time for talking is over. I should go and beat each and every one of them for their audacity!"

"Do as I say, boy!" Itosu blasted, but calmly added, "Go and talk to them and see if we can resolve this without violence. Tell them that I am with you and perhaps that will encourage them to leave us alone."

Funakoshi, embarrassed and ashamed at his disobedience, bowed once again to his master, apologized, and walked towards the men.

As Funakoshi approached the thuggish louts, their leader, 'The Brute', whose vision and, to some extent, bravado had until now been impaired by the moonlight, suddenly realized that he was being approached by what appeared to be a scrawny little lad. With this boost to his confidence, he stood a little taller, puffed out his chest, and splayed his arms in an aggressive posture meant to intimidate Funakoshi.

"I hope you've come to pay me, boy," The Brute growled, jutting his chin out to display his perceived superiority.

It took all Funakoshi's willpower and training not to land a punch onto that large target of a chin, but honouring Itosu's orders, he remained cool and spoke calmly. "I am afraid that we have no money, sir. My master, Anko Itosu, is asking if you would be so kind as to just let us on our way without any trouble, as we do not want to hurt any of you." Funakoshi could not resist adding the veiled threat.

The Brute burst into hysterical laughter and, turning to his cohorts, mocked, "He doesn't want to hurt any of us, he says. Look at him, the little runt couldn't hurt a fly!"

The bullying brute quickly spun back towards Funakoshi with a raised fist, thinking that he would frighten the boy. To his surprise, the lad had already dropped into a Karate stance with hands raised, ready to strike, and did not back away even an inch.

"Talk, Funakoshi!" Itosu's voice boomed from the distance.

Funakoshi relaxed and once more stood upright.

The Brute, whose ego had taken a bit of knock by this scrawny boy's total lack of fear, spoke again. "You should not interfere with adult matters, boy. Why doesn't your Master Itosu, whoever he is, speak to me himself? Is he such a coward that he has to hide behind the naïve bravery of small boys?"

That was the final straw for Funakoshi. Insulting him was one thing, but speaking of Master Itosu in such a disrespectful manner was another. Once again he dropped into a stance ready to strike.

Itosu again shouted, "No, Funakoshi!"

Before Funakoshi could disobey Itosu's orders, another group of drunk but very jolly men came stumbling around the corner, singing and laughing very loudly.

"Whoa! It looks like we've stumbled upon a fight!" one of the newcomers announced excitedly to his friends.

"Let's stay and watch a while. This could be fun!" another voice suggested in the darkness.

"Hold up a moment. I know that man. He is Itosu, the great Karate Master, and they are his students!" One of the new group stepped forward and approached Itosu. "It is you, Master Itosu, isn't it?' he asked.

"Hai," was the simple response from the great man.

The same man now turned towards the group of ruffians and shouted to them, "You guys must be crazy! Do you know who this is? This is Master Itosu, the greatest Karate Master in all Okinawa, and his students. They will give you the beating of your life! If I were you I'd apologize and be on my way."

The Brute looked once again at Funakoshi, shrugged his shoulders, and just grunted, "I've still never heard of him." Then, without any apology, he signalled to his gang that they should leave. Mumbling amongst themselves, they turned on their heels and disappeared back into the forest.

As soon as Funakoshi had rejoined them, Itosu took his students back home using an alternative route to ensure that they avoided any more trouble from the same men. This decision also perturbed young Funakoshi and his fellow students. They felt that they had come out on top, so why should they be inconvenienced by having to take a longer route back? It just didn't seem fair.

The next day, Master Itosu explained to Funakoshi and his fellow students the reasoning behind his decision the previous evening. "On noticing the gang, I told you all to keep your backs to the moon. With the moonlight behind us and shining directly into their eyes, they could not see very well, giving us a great advantage should physical confrontation have become necessary.

"I then asked Funakoshi to speak to their leader, as he is the smallest of you and would appear to be less of a threat to them, which further defused the situation. Funakoshi is also our best karateka and would be able to deal with any attack should it occur.

"Those same men have visited me this morning to apologize for their behaviour, and I have learned that they are untrained in any form of fighting. How would you feel today if last night you had just gone full steam ahead and beaten drunken and untrained men? It would have proven nothing at all. By taking an alternative route back, we ensured our safety and theirs, and who knows, they could have gone for reinforcements or even to pick up weapons.

"A true karateka should maintain constant zanshin [awareness] to be able to avoid confrontation. Last night we lost zanshin by losing track of time and put ourselves in peril by making our way home at too late an hour, when it is well known that drunks and thugs wander the countryside.

"Remember that Karate-Do is more than having the ability to win a fight. It is about recognizing danger and being able to avoid it without harm coming to anyone at all; it is about knowing your strengths and limitations; it is about knowing when to stand and fight and when to walk away; but above all, it is about justice and honour and doing the right thing. For those reasons, violence should never be resorted to lightly."

The lessons Funakoshi learned on that beautiful and, as it turned out, potentially dangerous moonlit summer's night had a profound effect on him. It could be that Itosu's words of wisdom inspired him to write his famous 'Twenty Precepts of Karate-Do'.

46
Gichin Funakoshi's Twenty Precepts of Karate-Do

As well as being an incredible karateka, Gichin Funakoshi was also a great thinker, philosopher and prolific writer. He believed that Karate-Do was much more than a physical exercise or means of self-defence. He saw Karate as a way of life that improved the entire person, physically, mentally, and spiritually.

Recognizing that this way of life was not an easy road to take, he wrote his Twenty Precepts as a guide for those wishing to be both a better karateka and a better person. Following are the Twenty Precepts along with a brief explanation of how each of them can apply to both Karate and to your everyday life.

1. KARATE BEGINS AND ENDS WITH COURTESY

Funakoshi's first and, we can assume, his most important rule.

Karate

Courtesy and respect are the foundation upon which Karate is built. One must bow on entering and leaving the dojo, and before and after kumite practice. Students must always show respect to higher grades and their Sensei by bowing and saying 'Oss' upon greeting them and upon receiving instructions from them to show that they have both listened and understood.

Everyday Life

A true karateka should always be courteous, respectful, and polite to others throughout their daily lives. In school, work, or at home, make every effort to show respect to those in authority, such as your teacher, parents, or employer. This respect will usually pay dividends.

2. THERE IS NO FIRST ATTACK IN KARATE—'KARATE NI SENTE NASHI'

Karate

Karate was created as a system of self-defence and must not be used to initiate an attack on another person. In kumite practice, the emphasis is always on defending oneself against an aggressor.

Everyday Life

The above rule applies to a real self-defence situation. However, a first attack could also mean a verbal threat. Therefore, if you feel that you or someone you care for are in danger of attack and all other means of escape have failed, then you should strike quickly to aid your escape.

It could also mean that we should look, listen, and study before making comment or judgement about something or someone.

3. KARATE IS AN AID TO JUSTICE

Karate

A true karateka only ever uses his skills to defend himself or someone else. Karate should be taught responsibly to create honest and honourable human beings. In the dojo, as in life, using Karate to hurt or bully another person is absolutely not tolerated.

Everyday Life

Karate-Do teaches us to care not only for ourselves but to look out for others. This does not just mean using Karate skills to help somebody in danger from another person. It also implies that we should give our help to those who need it in any way we can.

4. FIRST CONTROL YOURSELF BEFORE ATTEMPTING TO CONTROL OTHERS

Karate

Learning Karate-Do requires a huge amount of dedication and self-discipline. Having to train two or three times a week, practising the same technique or kata repeatedly for many months or even years, takes real staying power. No excuses to skip lessons should be acceptable, and when attending lessons, one hundred per cent effort should be given to every exercise, no matter how many times it may have to be repeated. A karateka with this level of self-discipline will go far and perhaps progress to teaching others.

Everyday Life

Life requires the same dedication and self-control that Karate teaches. Doing homework, chores, or your job to the best of your ability every day takes self-discipline. To say no to your friends when you know that what they are doing is wrong takes a huge amount of self-discipline and courage. To eat the right food and ignore that tasty burger, to say no to cigarettes, alcohol, and drugs all take immense self-discipline. Only when you can control your own body and mind do you have the right to help and give advice to others about how to control theirs.

5. SPIRIT BEFORE TECHNIQUE

Karate

Always give one hundred per cent effort to every technique when practising Karate. An imperfect technique performed with spirit is still more effective than a perfect technique performed with no power or feeling.

Everyday Life

Whatever sport or activity you do—schoolwork, your job, or even friendships—the greater the effort you put in, the greater the reward you get back.

6. ALWAYS BE READY TO RELEASE YOUR MIND

Karate

Through your Karate career you may have the privilege of training with many different instructors, perhaps from many different styles and arts. If you become set in your ways, believing that your way is the only way, you are denying yourself the chance to develop and grow as a more complete martial artist. No matter how long you have trained or how good you may be, there is always more to learn. Observe, learn, and take from others the things that work for you, and do not disregard anything offhand.

Everyday Life

In all aspects of life we have to grow and adapt to survive. Just because you've been shown one way to do something doesn't mean that it is the only or best way of doing it. Listen to, read about, watch, and copy how other people do things. Then experiment with your own ideas and you can make an informed and educated choice of what is best for you.

7. ACCIDENTS ARISE FROM NEGLIGENCE

Karate

In the dojo there are strict rules for everyone's safety. Only ever practise what your Sensei has shown you, and when he gives the command to stop, do so immediately. Do not lose concentration during Karate practice, as this can lead to accidents.

Everyday Life

Can be a very dangerous thing. From boiling the kettle to crossing the road, every day we have to make thousands of decisions that could effect both ourselves and others in both the short and long term. Always act responsibly and thoughtfully, as negligence and irresponsibility could prove to be disastrous.

8. DO NOT THINK THAT KARATE TRAINING IS ONLY FOR THE DOJO

Karate

Karate requires very little time or space to be practised. It can take less than a minute to perform a whole kata. Do not wait for your next lesson before practising what you learned in the previous one. The more you practise, the quicker you can be assessed, and your Sensei can move on to newer aspects of your training.

Everyday Life

Every aspect of life requires practise and hard work, and even occasional failure for us to become to become good at it. This is why your teachers give you homework and why your parents give you chores. To be prepared for a full and productive life requires constant practise and work.

9. IT WILL TAKE YOUR ENTIRE LIFE TO LEARN KARATE; THERE IS NO LIMIT

Karate

Many karateka seem to believe that once they have attained a 1st Dan, the much-coveted black belt, they have learned everything they need to know about Karate. This could not be further from the truth! Although it is a great achievement, at 1st Dan level a student has only just begun to gain an understanding of Karate basics. I don't believe that any one person could ever fully grasp the full scope of what Karate has to show us. I have been a practising karateka for forty years, and I am still learning something new every day and will continue to do so for as long as I continue in Karate.

Everyday Life

Life itself is a continuous and infinite learning process, with new experiences and challenges occurring practically every minute of every day. We have to embrace these experiences and challenges, learn from our mistakes, and try and try and try again to learn and develop as people.

10. PUT YOUR EVERYDAY LIVING INTO KARATE AND YOU WILL FIND MYO

Karate and Everyday Life

'Myo' means to reach a level of outstanding skill and understanding. Funakoshi believed that only way to attain myo is for a karateka to see no boundaries or difference between the way he behaves in the dojo and the way he conducts himself in everyday life. The same incredibly high levels of discipline, courtesy, and respect should be maintained at all times.

11. KARATE IS LIKE BOILING WATER: IF YOU DO NOT HEAT IT CONSTANTLY, IT WILL COOL DOWN

Karate

You cannot hope to learn Karate by practising once a week or every now and then. You will soon find that your fellow students have surpassed your knowledge and skill levels, and you are being left behind. As with precept No.8, you must constantly fuel the fire of your training, or it will simply burn out and be reduced to ash. You then have start again by rebuilding the fire before you can get the benefit of the heat. Practise, practise, practise!

Everyday Life

The same rule applies to every aspect of your daily life. If you have a school or work project, do not leave it until the last minute, as you may find that you have forgotten what you were supposed to do in the first place. Relationships with family and friends, perhaps more than anything else, require constant attention and work to maintain. If you haven't seen someone in a while, just pick up the phone and say hello. This is often all that's needed to keep the fires of friendship burning brightly.

12. Do not think that you have to win; think rather that you do not have to lose

Karate

A true karateka should accept both victory and defeat honourably and graciously. Whilst winning a tournament or passing a grading first time is reason for celebration, every match whether you win or lose, and every grading whether you pass or fail, is an opportunity to learn from mistakes, improve, and prepare for next time.

Everyday Life

A true karateka should always maintain constant 'zanshin' (awareness) to recognize and avoid potentially dangerous or violent situations. If for any reason confrontation is unavoidable, always try to talk the situation down without resorting to physical force. Without having to win a physical battle, you will have avoided losing a fight or possibly your life.

In all areas of your life, for example if you did not get the grade you expected in an exam, or you weren't selected for the soccer team, find out where you made mistakes and how to learn and improve so you do better next time around.

13. Victory depends on your ability to distinguish vulnerable points from invulnerable ones

Karate

In Karate competition you should study your opponents to find out how to best use your strengths against their weaknesses. Often these observations must be made in a split second during the fight. By studying your opponent's hand, feet, and body position, you will soon learn to recognize where his attack may come from and how to react and win.

Everyday Life

Every difficult task in life should be thought about and planned for to make it as easy as possible, for example exams require you to revise and study, with extra special attention given to your weaker subjects. With thought and careful planning you can achieve anything.

14. THE BATTLE IS ACCORDING TO HOW YOU MOVE: GUARDED OR UNGUARDED

Karate

Following on from No.13, this precept tells us to adapt our fighting style according to your opponent's movements. If you have a cautious opponent who is waiting for you to move, use feints or pretence, drawing him in by briefly opening your guard. When your opponent reacts to your trap, exploit the opening to score. If your opponent is aggressive, fast, and elusive, ensure your guard is effective and use caution and patience. This kind of fighter always leaves himself exposed for your counter at some point.

Everyday Life

You should always maintain a guard of awareness and alertness throughout life to protect yourself physically, mentally, and emotionally. Although this guard should never be completely dropped, it is essential to relax it occasionally to build healthy friendships and relationships.

15. THINK OF YOUR HANDS AND FEET AS SWORDS

Karate

Karate-Do, is 'the way of the empty hand', using only the body as a weapon, with the hands and feet as the primary striking tools. During all aspects of training, you should imagine your hands and feet striking and finishing an opponent with one blow, as would a sword.

Everyday Life

As well as maintaining constant zanshin, you should always project the appearance of confidence and ability, even if you do not as yet truly possess those qualities. A confident and alert person is not a desirable target to a potential attacker, so walk as proudly as a samurai warrior.

16. WHEN YOU LEAVE YOUR HOME, THINK THAT YOU HAVE NUMEROUS OPPONENTS WAITING FOR YOU

Karate

It's that old favourite zanshin (awareness) again. During your Karate lesson you should think of all your fellow students as potential attackers, whether you are doing partner work or not. Training your zanshin in a safe environment like your dojo will help prepare you for the real world.

Everyday Life

As soon as you step outside your home for school, work, or play, you should be prepared at all times for potential dangers, such as when crossing the road, avoiding trouble, and not talking to strangers. There are more tips in the chapter on self-protection.

17. Beginners must master low stance and posture; natural body positions are for the advanced

Karate

Stance is the foundation of strong Karate technique. Beginners have to practise low, strong, and physically demanding stances. This builds leg strength, good posture, and a strong foundation from which to build and increase your skill levels. Once the stances have been mastered, a more natural posture can be assumed, particularly during kumite, to allow greater speed and freedom of movement.

Everyday Life

It is a human trait that many of us want to run before we can walk when learning new skills. This is particularly true of children and young adults. If you are a child or young adult reading this, I expect that at some time or another you have felt hard done by with a parent or teacher who has not allowed you the freedom you feel you deserve. As in Karate, life requires a firm, strong foundation to develop and grow healthily. Try to understand that your parents and other adults responsible for your well-being are acting for your safety and best interests. With guidance, you will grow and develop responsibly, and then in time you will earn their trust and the freedom to make your own choices.

18. Practising kata is one thing; engaging in a real fight is another

Karate

It would be foolish to believe that having mastered several kata, you suddenly become an adept fighter. Kata are very ordered and neat patterns, whereas real fights are messy and chaotic affairs which should be avoided at all times. The only way to prepare for the reality of fighting is to introduce realistic elements and attacks into your partner training, and study how the techniques found in kata can be applied practically.

Everyday Life

Just because you've read a cookery book doesn't make you a great chef. You then have to go out and buy the ingredients, follow the recipe, and try to cook the meal. With practise you will be able to cook without the recipe and may even improve upon it. To have success with anything in life requires constant hard work and practise.

19. DO NOT FORGET TO CORRECTLY APPLY STRENGTH AND WEAKNESS OF POWER; STRETCHING AND CONTRACTION OF THE BODY; AND SLOWNESS AND SPEED OF TECHNIQUES

Karate

With time you will come to understand how to read your opponent's movements and use them to your benefit. Sometimes it will require all your strength, speed and power to win a fight. At other times you'll be able to use your opponent's momentum to easily overcome him with the lightest of touches, such as when Azato fought the great swordsman Yorin Kanna.

Everyday Life

Every day of our lives we have to make decisions, which are sometimes difficult for us, and likewise, other people have to make decisions for us that we may not agree with. Imagine that you wanted to stay out until midnight with your friends, and your parents did not find this acceptable. Would it be best to immediately fly into a hissy-fit before your parents can continue any further? Or would it be wiser to remain cool and calm and negotiate a possible compromise? Depending on your reaction, you could, on the one hand, find yourself grounded for a month for unacceptable behaviour, or on the other hand, perhaps out with your friends until a mutually acceptable time. Learn how to behave and react sensibly with other people.

20. ALWAYS THINK AND DEVISE WAYS TO LIVE THE PRECEPTS EVERY DAY

Karate

The Twenty Precepts are an essential guide to being a good or even a great karateka. Remember that the concepts of courtesy, discipline, and hard work are at the very heart of Karate-Do.

Everyday Life

The Twenty Precepts, as we have studied throughout this section, can teach us all, karateka or not, how to be good, decent people. This section has only scratched the surface of how the twenty precepts relate to us in everyday life. So do as No.20 advises and look for ways to live the precepts every moment of every day.

47
Gichin Funakoshi—The Father of Modern Karate-Do

Gichin Funakoshi was involved in so many Karate firsts and achieved so much in the promotion of Karate throughout the world that to write in length about them all would require another book! If you'd like to find out more about this great man, I highly recommend that you read his biography *Karate-Do: My Way of Life*.

Following in date order are just some of the many achievements of this great man, who because of his integral role in enabling the global spread of Karate, became fondly referred to as The Father of Modern Karate-Do.

THE ACHIEVEMENTS OF GICHIN 'SHOTO' FUNAKOSHI

1902—Under the watchful eye and guidance of his great mentor Itosu, Funakoshi held the first public demonstration of Karate at his school. The school authorities were so impressed at the physical fitness of the participants that by 1905, Karate was being taught throughout many schools on Okinawa.

1912—Funakoshi gave a demonstration of Karate to officers of the Japanese Imperial Navy fleet. The senior officers were so stunned at the physique and fitness of the karateka that they sent crewmen to learn Karate with Funakoshi. From 1912 until 1921, Funakoshi and other prominent karateka increased the growing popularity of Karate by holding many demonstrations throughout Okinawa.

1921—Gichin Funakoshi can't believe his luck when a request from Crown Prince Hirohito of Japan is sent to him requesting a demonstration of Karate in the great hall of Shuri Castle. The Prince was amazed at the incredible skills on display, and Funakoshi was asked to introduce Karate to the Japanese mainland. Funakoshi agreed, and to aid his mission in Japan, he created the very first photographic record of Karate, which he placed on a scroll.

Leaving his beloved wife and family in Okinawa, Funakoshi set sail for Japan, expecting to be home in a few months. He did not return to Okinawa or see his wife for nearly twenty years.

1922—Funakoshi gave the very first demonstration of Karate on the Japanese mainland in the Women's Higher Normal School in Tokyo. This was followed by many more, including one for the great Judo Master Jigoro Kano at the famous Kodokan dojo. Kano was so intrigued with this Okinawan martial art that he asked Funakoshi, who was due to return home, to teach him Karate. Although Funakoshi desperately missed his wife, he could not refuse the great man, and so began the chain of delays that was to keep him in Japan for the rest of his life.

In the same year, Funakoshi completed the first ever reference book of Karate, *Ryukyu Kempo: Tode*. Tragically, the printing plates for this book were destroyed in a terrible earthquake that devastated a large area of Japan the following year. Not easily deterred, Funakoshi set about improving the original and completed *Renten Goshin Tode—Jutsu* in 1925. Then, in 1935, he completed the most influential and important Karate manual in the history of the art, *Karate Do Kyohan*. As well as extensively recording Karate in his books, Funakoshi was the first man to put Karate onto film.

1936—A proud Funakoshi stepped across the threshold of his now world famous dojo, named the Shotokan in his honour. Shoto was the name he used as a young man to sign his poetry and 'kan' simply means 'hall'. Shotokan was to become the name for the type of Karate Funakoshi taught and is now the most widely practised Karate style in the world with over five million practitioners.

During the terrible years of World War II that followed, much of Japan was devastated. Many of Funakoshi's young students went off to fight for Japan and never returned, and his beloved Shotokan Dojo was destroyed during a bombing raid. Funakoshi was finally reunited with his wife after she fled war-torn Okinawa. Sadly, she died from chronic asthma shortly after.

Despite all the horrors of war, the tragedy of family loss, and his advancing years, Gichin Funakoshi remained focused on his goal to see Karate's worldwide acceptance. This was assured when in the 1950s he presented Karate demonstrations to the American armed forces. Some of these servicemen went on to learn Karate and took it back home, where they opened their own schools in the United States.

This was still not enough for Funakoshi, as the last sentence of his biography, *Karate Do: My Way of Life*, illustrates. He says:

"Still astonished by the number of people who have heard of Karate, I now realize that once this book is finished I shall have to start a new project—that of sending Japanese experts abroad."

True to his word, he sent some of the greatest karateka in the world to America and Europe to spread the word of Karate. Today, over five million people in nearly seventy countries practise Shotokan Karate, plus millions more in other variations of the art.

Gichin Funakoshi, The Father of Modern Karate, died in 1957 aged eighty-nine.

48
Modern Masters—You Could Be One!

You may or may not be surprized to learn that all of the amazing past Masters of Karate that we have discussed were just normal people like you and me. However, once they had discovered their passion and the direction in life they wanted to take, they did so with absolute commitment. Each one of them had their own reason and motivation for being the best martial artist they could be: religious discipline, revenge, protecting others, and, in the case of Funakoshi, ensuring that Karate survived to become one of the most practised pastimes in the world.

Your motivation does not need to be as grand as that of Funakoshi or the other old Masters. Your goal could be to attain a black belt, be club champion, or simply to get fit, which are all fantastic objectives, and with hard work you could soon achieve them.

On the other hand, you may want to become an instructor, or long to be a world champion. These are amazing goals that are still absolutely achievable as long as you are willing and able to put in the incredibly hard work required to attain them. There will be people that will tell you that you are mad to even dream of achieving such great things, and there will be people who will support you all the way.

Since Karate gained worldwide recognition, there have been several influential karateka from around the world that could certainly be classed as modern Karate Masters. So work and train as hard as you can and ignore the knockers and the doubters. Surround yourself with positive and supportive friends and family, and you never know; you just might be the next Gichin Funakoshi or Anko Itosu.

Part III

Useful Information for You

49
Practical Self-Protection for the Whole Family

Throughout this book you will have noticed the word 'zanshin' repeated many times. Zanshin means 'awareness', which is the key to effective self-protection. Although awareness requires no punchbags or stretching, it does require constant practice. By training your eyes, ears, and brain to recognize possibly dangerous situations, you will learn to avoid hazards and keep yourself safe from harm without having to resort to physical action.

Simply believing that just because you practise a martial art you will be able to defend yourself from any attacker is extremely foolhardy and dangerous. This is especially true of more vulnerable people such as children. The best self-protection skills are those that teach you to avoid trouble altogether.

Following are just a few simple and practical self-protection tips for everyone that you should try to practise at all times:

1. Always listen to your parents, as they love and care for you more than anybody else.
2. If you are going out, make sure someone knows where you are going, what route you are taking to get there, and what time you will be back.
3. Carry a cell phone! Even if it doesn't work, a potential attacker will think twice if you are apparently talking on the phone.
4. In school, always listen to your teachers, as they have your best interest at heart.
5. Never talk to strangers.
6. Do not associate with troublemakers, either in or outside of school.
7. If possible, never be outside alone.
8. Stay away from secluded areas, even if it is a short cut. Better to arrive late than not at all.
9. Always try to walk down the middle of a pavement, a safe distance from the road and away from property entrances, which can hide possible danger.
10. Always walk towards oncoming traffic so that you can see if a car slows down or stops.
11. If someone asks directions from a car, stay well away from the window and out of arm's reach.
12. If you stop to ask for directions in your car, only lower the window a couple of inches.
13. When you leave your house, school, etc., always check up and down the road for anything suspicious.

14. When approaching your house or car, have the keys ready so you do not have to fumble around in your pocket or bag.

15. Finally, and most importantly, if anyone is hurting you or asking you to do something you know to be wrong, TELL SOMEONE YOU TRUST! Your parents, another family member, or a police officer; tell a teacher, a friend, a friend's parents, or even your Karate instructor. They will believe you and help you to resolve the situation, whatever it may be.

Your eyes, ears, and brain are the most effective weapons in self-protection!

50
Karate Terminology

When you first take up Karate, you may suddenly be confronted with an instructor that appears to be speaking complete and utter gobbledygook. Don't panic; the instructor is not crazy, like King Sho Ko. Sensei is using Japanese words that will soon become very familiar to you. This section has been included as a reference to help you learn the most commonly used words and phrases.

PARTS OF THE BODY

Ashi	Foot/leg
Ashikubi	Ankle
Ashi yubi	Toes
Chudan	Torso/middle level
Empi	Elbow
Gan	Eye
Gedan	Lower body/lower level
Hai-wan	Back of the arm
Hara	Abdomen
Hidari	Left
Jodan	Head/upper level
Hiza	Knee or lap

Kakato	Heel of the foot
Kami	Hair
Kansetsu	Joint
Komekami	Temple
Koshi	Ball of the foot
Kubi	Neck
Men	Face
Migi	Right
Mimi	Ear
Momo	Thigh
Mune	Chest
Seiken	Fist
Seoi	Shoulder
Shofu	Side of the neck
Sokko	Instep
Sokuto	Edge of the foot
Te	Hand
Ude	Forearm
Wan	Arm
Yoko	Side

DACHI—STANCES

Fudo dachi	Immovable stance
Gankaku dachi	Crane stance
Hachiji dachi	Open leg stance
Hangetsu dachi	Half-moon stance
Heiko dachi	Parallel stance
Heisoku dachi	Informal stance
Kiba dachi	Straddle/horseback stance
Kokutsa dachi	Back stance
Kosa dachi	Cross stance
Musubi dachi	Informal stance
Neko-Ashi dachi	Cat's foot stance
Renoji dachi	L stance
Sanchin dachi	Hourglass stance

Shiko dachi	Square stance
Shizen dachi	Natural stance
Sochin dachi	Diagonal straddle stance
Tachi	Standing or stance
Teiji dachi	T-Shape stance
Tsuri Ashi dachi	Crane stance
Zenkutsu dachi	Front stance

TSUKI—FIST THRUSTS OR PUNCHES

Age tsuki	Rising punch
Awase tsuki	Combined punch
Choku tsuki	Straight punch
Dan tsuki	Consecutive punch (same hand)
Gyaku tsuki	Reverse punch
Hiraken	Flat fist
Kage tsuki	Hooked punch
Kizami tsuki	Jabbing punch
Mawashi tsuki	Roundhouse punch
Oi tsuki	Lunging punch
Sanbon tsuki	Three punches
Seijen	Regular fist
Tate zuke	Vertical punch
Ura tsuki	Short punch
Yama zuki	Wide 'U' punch

UKE—BLOCK OR RECEIVING TECHNIQUES

Age uke	Rising block
Awase uke	Combined block
Gedan uke	Downward sweeping block
Gedan berai	Downward block
Hai-wan uke	Back arm block
Juji uke	X block
Kaisho uke	Open hand block
Kakiwake uke	Wedge block
Keito uke	Chicken head block

Morote uke	Augmented block
Nagashi uke	Sweeping block
Otoshi uke	Dropping block
Shuto uke	Knife hand block
Soto uke	Outside block
Uchi uke	Inside block
Ude uke	Forearm block

UCHI—STRIKES

Age empi uchi	Upward elbow
Empi uchi	Elbow strike
Haishu uchi	Backhand strike
Haito uchi	Ridge-hand strike
Kakato uchi	Bent wrist strike
Keito uchi	Chicken head strike
Nukite	Spear hand
Shuto uchi	Knife hand strike
Teisho uchi	Palm heal strike
Tettsui uchi	Hammer fist strike
Uraken uchi	Back fist strike
Washide uchi	Eagle beak strike
Yoko empi	Side elbow strike

OTHER TERMINOLOGY

Age	Rising
Aka	Red
Ao	Blue
Awase	Combined
Budo	Martial way
Bushido	Way of the warrior
Dan	Level
Do	The way
Dojo	Place of training
Enoy	Relax
Gawa	Side

Gi	Uniform
Gyaku	Reverse
Hai	Yes
Hajime	Start/begin
Hanmi	Half-front
Hara	Abdomen
Hiki	Pulling
Hyosh	Timing
Iee Lie	No
Ippon	One point
Ka	Practitioner
Kaiten	Rotating
Kara	Empty
Kata	Form
Kiai	Spirit breath/shout
Kime	Focus
Kohai	Junior
Kumite	Fighting
Mae	Front
Mawate	Turn
Miru	Look
Obi	Belt
Oss	Understanding
Otoshi	Dropping
Rei	Bow
Ryo	Both
Ryu	School of martial arts
Seiza	Kneeling position
Sempai	Senior
Sensei	Teacher
Shihan	Master
Tai sabaki	Body movement
Te	Hand
Tobi	Jumping
Yame	Return to ready position
Yoi	Prepare

Yoko		Side	
Zanshin		Alertness/awareness	

NUMBERS

One	Ichi	**Eleven**	Jyu ichi
Two	Ni	**Twelve**	Jyu ni
Three	San	**Thirteen**	Jyu san
Four	Shi	**Fourteen**	Jyu shi
Five	Go	**Fifteen**	Jyu go
Six	Roku	**Sixteen**	Jyu roku
Seven	Sichi	**Seventeen**	Jyu sichi
Eight	Hachi	**Eighteen**	Jyu hachi
Nine	Ku	**Nineteen**	Jyu ku
Ten	Ju	**Twenty**	Ni ju

KATA NAMES AND TRANSLATIONS

The translations below are the most commonly used. As you come to learn more about the history of Karate, you will discover that these translations are not literal and that each kata name can be interpreted in several ways. The kata names outside the brackets are those used in the style that I practice, Shotokan. The kata names within the brackets are the original Chinese/Okinawan names, which are still used by other styles like Wado Ryu.

Bassai Dai	(Patsai)	To Storm a Castle/Fortress
Bassai Sho		Storm a Fortress (minor)
Chinte		Rare Hand
Empi	(Wanshu)	Swallow in Flight
Gankaku	(Chinto)	Crane on the Rock
Gojoshihio Dai		Fifty-Four Steps (minor)

Gojoshihosho		Fifty-Four Steps (major)
Hangetsu	**(Seisan)**	Half-Moon
Heian 1:5	**(Pinan)**	Peaceful Mind/Safe From Harm
Ji'in		Temple Grounds
Jion		Kind and Gentle
Jitte		Ten Hands
Kanku Dai	**(Kushanku)**	To View the Sky
Kanku Sho		To View the Sky (major)
Meikyo	**(Rohai)**	Polished Mirror
Nijushiho	**(Niseishi)**	Twenty-Four Steps
Sochin		Immovable Force
Tekki Nidan		Iron Horse 2
Tekki Sandan		Iron Horse 3
Tekki Shodan	**(Naihanchi)**	Iron Horse
Unsu		Hands in the Clouds
Wankan Sho		King's Crown

51
Dojo Etiquette/Rules

Karate has strict rules for behaviour and appearance that should be adhered to whenever you attend training at your dojo. These rules will vary slightly from dojo to dojo but are all very similar. The rules of etiquette for my dojo are:

1. You must always bow when entering and leaving the dojo.
2. You must always address your instructors as Sensei in the dojo, no matter how friendly you may be outside.
3. You should always bow and say 'oss' to your Sensei when:
   - You first enter the dojo at the beginning of a lesson
   - On receiving instruction
   - At the end of your lesson before leaving the dojo.
4. You should always bow and say 'oss' to your partner before and after kumite practice.
5. You cannot leave the lesson for any reason without your Sensei's permission.
6. You cannot rejoin the lesson without your Sensei's permission.

7. You must always arrive on time for your lesson.

8. If you arrive late, you must kneel and wait for your Sensei's permission to enter. On Sensei's invitation, you should then walk around the back of the class, NOT THROUGH IT!

9. You must be washed and clean for your lesson, especially your hands and feet.

10. You cannot wear any jewellery or watches during a lesson.

11. You must always wear a clean and pressed gi.

12. Do not chew gum or bring snacks to class. Only hydrating drinks are allowed or required.

13. You cannot attend a lesson if you have consumed any alcohol.

14. No offensive behaviour, i.e. spitting, swearing, and bullying, is tolerated in the dojo.

15. Anyone found to be using Karate outside the dojo for any other reason than self-defence or practise will be banned from the class.

16. NEVER talk when your Sensei is speaking or when you should be practising.

17. If you wish to ask a question you must raise your hand.

18. Do not come to the dojo to watch if you are injured or sick without first asking permission from your Sensei. If you can make it to the dojo you can train! You will never be asked to do anything you are not capable of. If the reason for not training is financial, talk to your instructor.

19. If you are asked to sit whilst other grades train, do not treat it as a break! Sit quietly and concentrate on what they are doing.

20. Regular attendance at lessons does not guarantee that you will pass your grading. It is up to you to train hard and reach the required standards.

21. Always train to the best of your ability and embrace the spirit of Karate-Do at all times.

THE END